Sci ✓

B1P.167
1 x 1/69
1/6~

FY2/05...167
27 x 8/11 1/12 B1r

D1164748

The Advertising Agency Business

The Advertising Agency Business

The Complete Manual for Management & Operation

Third Edition

Eugene J. Hameroff

NTC Business Books

NTC/Contemporary Publishing Group

Library of Congress Cataloging-in-Publication Data

Hameroff, Eugene J.
    The advertising agency business : the complete manual for
management & operation / Eugene J. Hameroff. — 3rd ed.
       p.   cm.
    Rev. ed. of: The advertising agency business / Herbert S.
Gardner. 1988.
    Includes index.
    ISBN 0-8442-3169-X
    1. Advertising agencies—United States—Management.
I. Gardner, Herbert S. Advertising agency business.   II. Title.
HF6178.H347   1997
659.1'125'068—dc21   97-37330
                                            CIP

Published by NTC Business Books
An imprint of NTC/Contemporary Publishing Company
4255 West Touhy Avenue, Lincolnwood (Chicago), Illinois 60646-1975 U.S.A.
Copyright © 1998, 1988 by NTC/Contemporary Publishing Company
Printed in the United States of America
International Standard Book Number: 0-8442-3169-X

18   17   16   15   14   13   12   11   10   9   8   7   6   5   4   3   2

Contents

Acknowledgments

First, I would like to acknowledge you, my dear reader, for showing the interest in starting your own agency. It's a wonderful feeling to go into business for yourself, and you will find a world of satisfaction in carving out your own destiny. I'm happy to see that the entrepreneurial spirit is alive and well.

The agency business offers an exciting and stimulating challenge and can be very rewarding, emotionally and financially. Of course there will be problems along the way, and my purpose in bringing this book to you is to help you level out the playing field and help you to create a thriving, successful agency, doing good work for clients—and getting well paid for it.

And, of course, my thanks also go to Herb Gardner, who wrote the original edition of this book. Mr. Gardner was the financial guru of the advertising agency business—he helped put the financial butterflies into formation for countless agencies. We have revised and updated the material, written many years ago, to keep up with the fast-changing advertising and marketing explosion that is now taking place.

And as a final acknowledgment, I want to thank my partner, Pete Lustig, who provided substantial material on computers, the Internet, and new business techniques. His help and advice have been invaluable.

You are now entering a new world. Stick with the basics of good management, work hard to keep your clients happy, and you will succeed and prosper beyond your wildest dreams. It's all out there.

— Introduction —

Welcome to the Brave New World of the Advertising Agency Business

The latest figures available when *The Advertising Agency Business* was revised in 1988 recorded that 95.1 billion dollars were spent on advertising in the United States.

But, how things have changed since the last time this book was revised!

In its annual report of advertising expenditures, McCann-Erickson estimated that this figure had grown to $161.5 billion by 1995.

Based on statistics from the Bureau of Labor, Office of Employment Statistics, the total number of employees working in advertising agencies was reported to be 166,300 in 1995. The largest agencies employed as many as five thousand, while the smallest, of course, were the one-person shops—those just getting started or choosing to remain one-person shops. The report shows that there were 243,000 employees in all of advertising.

Adding to the confusion is the fact that the term "advertising agency" is often used very loosely. For instance, the latest available figures from American Business Marketing, a leading list broker, indicates that there are 24,632 "advertising agencies" in the United States. However, our own experience in buying lists from list brokers shows graphic art studios, tattoo parlors, freelancers, public relations firms, individual artists, marketing organizations, publishers, and many other entities listed as advertising agencies.

Not only have expenditures exploded—so has the number of options for the way advertising money can be spent. New media have emerged and some minor media of the last decade have become major media today. Among them are cable television advertising, new forms of direct marketing, and, of course, the Internet.

THE INTERNET ARRIVES

The Internet is a prime example of the new challenges that growth and change present to operators of advertising agencies. This medium offers an opportunity upon which agencies can capitalize. However, it also calls for new marketing communications strategies, the employment of graphics and computer specialists, retraining of media planners and buyers, etc.

Since 1988, there have been other notable changes in media. The basic three television networks have been supplemented by additional networks. Cable channels have burgeoned to where there are currently more than five hundred cable services to choose from. Specialized magazines have become the lifeline of publishers, and now advertisers have a choice of hundreds.

The changes that affect advertising agency operations are by no means limited to the media scene. The use of fax machines has revised agency operational procedures, CD-ROM technology has opened a new path for communications, and cellular telephones and E-mail have increased the scope and flexibility of agency operators.

These communications technology developments have increased the reach of local advertising agencies, making them national and even global. It is quite common for nonbranch agencies to handle clients located hundreds or thousands of miles away.

National and international networks of independent advertising agencies have grown. These voluntary networks have made member agency operators competitive with the multinational agencies.

AGENCY NAMES HAVE GONE THROUGH THE REVOLVING DOOR

Taking a broader view of what has occurred in the advertising world over the last decade, we see that megamergers have brought former agency adversaries together to form communications giants. Mergers have also united telephone companies and cable TV firms. Broadcasting networks have tied in with movie studios.

As of this writing, here are some of the changes and acquisitions that have taken place in the world of advertising agencies:

Ross Roy to Omnicom as part of DAS (Diversified Agency Services) division

Chiat/Day to Omnicom's TBWA to form TBWA/Chiat Day

Kobs & Draft leaves Cordiant (Saatchi) in a leveraged buyout (LBO) to form DraftDirect

Campbell Mithun Esty leaves Cordiant in LBO (with 50 percent of equity taken by IPG)

Griffin Bacal bought by Omnicom for its DDB Needham arm

Floathe Johnson bought by EvansGroup

Ketchum Communications bought January '95 by Omnicom

Bayer Bess Vanderwarker bought by True North

Altschiller & Co. bought by Hill Holliday Connors Cosmopulos

Anderson & Lembke bought by IPG

Addison Whitney bought by IPG

Ammirati & Puris bought (in late '93) by IPG for its Lintas arm; that arm is now called Ammirati Puris Lintas

Bloom FCA became Publicis/Bloom when Publicis S.A., Paris, bought Bloom parent, FCA, Paris

Dugan Farley bought by BJK&E from '95 bankruptcy victim, Ally & Gargano

Computerization has also changed creative capabilities. Where art departments formerly featured drawing boards and hand-drawn work, today one sees artists doing all of their creating with computer software. Jobs that used to take days to complete are now done in hours.

All of this growth and change has strongly affected the competitive aspects of the agency business. The old days of placing a newspaper ad or running some broadcast spots and then waiting to see what happens are over. Today's merchandising tactics could be characterized as street fighting—and marketing communications as the weapons. The combat includes cross merchandising, an overkill of telemarketing, and a proliferation of couponing. This environment makes the business of handling clients more intensely competitive and complicated.

Although this book is about the business side of running an advertising agency, the way an agency operator utilizes the myriad advertising vehicles and the advanced technologies can dramatically affect the agency's profitability and growth.

The advertising business is always on the leading edge of change in a rapidly changing world. Those who have elected to become part of the agency business must therefore be perpetually contemporary in their mindsets and their use of newly developing resources.

ABOUT THIS BOOK

The previous version of this book was written in 1988 by Herb Gardner, Jr., and reflected agency operations at the time. Herb had a distinguished, stellar career in agency management, having worked as consultant, chief financial officer of a major agency, and as managing director of two agency networks.

In response to the many momentous changes taking place in the nineties in the speed of communications, the new and unprecedented techniques of how to get new clients, and the way this all affects the management and the bottom line of advertising agencies, the author has been given the privilege of updating the material. As Tevye, the harassed hero in the wonderful Broadway play *Fiddler on the Roof*, says to his wife, Goldie, "It's a new world out there . . . everything has changed," so it has with running an agency in the nineties and rushing toward the twenty-first century.

While maintaining the flavor and the philosophy of the role of advertising that Gardner has expounded, this book will show you, step by step, how to run a profitable agency in this new, fast-changing world.

Let's go to work and find out what it takes to run a successful advertising agency!

—Part I—

Advertising Agency Fundamentals

— 1 —

The Philosophy of Success

As I travel throughout the country consulting with small agencies, the owners always ask: "Why can't I find someone like me, who will work just as hard and be as dedicated to the success of this agency?"

My response usually is that if an employee had the same drive, ambition, and entrepreneurial spirit that you do, that employee would have his or her name on the door and own the place. That is not to say that employees in small agencies are not ambitious or dedicated, but it takes a special risk-taking quality to make the leap from employee to owner.

Starting and building an agency from conception to full-blown maturity requires a special breed of individual—someone who doesn't believe others who say it can't be done, someone who sees opportunity in every problem, someone who won't take "no" for an answer.

Besides the obvious necessary talents—like an intuitive creative process and a basic knowledge of how to handle money and people—success takes just what is needed in running any business: single-mindedness, determination, long hours, dedication, a focus on success, ability to overcome obstacles, and having the skill and patience to direct and handle some highly talented and temperamental staff members.

Quite a list!

If you think you can do it all by yourself, great! But growing your own agency offers significant challenges and rewards.

What does it take to bring success to an advertising agency? Certainly an agency must have sound procedures, a reasonable amount of billing, and adequate financial resources. Without them no business can succeed.

The necessary additional ingredient is a basic philosophy of business encompassing the two attributes that enable an agency to grow and prosper. These are *attitude* and *ability*. Neither by itself is sufficient. Both are needed and of the two, a proper attitude is much rarer.

What It Takes to Succeed

It is important for a young agency to realize that it cannot hold and build business just by copywriting ability, good art work, or even ingenuity in promotional ideas, however good they are. All these abilities are important, but they are not fundamental. Without basic sound selling judgment, the other abilities amount to nothing but fireworks with which to please and impress the client—and clients have an unpleasant habit of waking up from these dreams of greatness. Cleverness and ingenuity are a dime a dozen in our business and are often confused with ability. Actually, ability should enable the young agency operator to see these talents in their proper light, as a means rather than an end. Ability should give him good business judgment about his own operation, as well as those he endeavors to guide. Finally, real ability will dictate a proper attitude to the agency operator.

And what is this proper attitude? Well, for want of a better term, let's call it professionalism.

Just as a physician's whole aim is to cure a patient or, better yet, by proper preventive care keep an illness from occurring in the first place, an agency's aim should be to improve the client's position and swell his profits by increasing sales, decreasing costs, or a combination of the two.

The agency must be in a position to give its client good business advice and to do so *it must know more about advertising than its client does.* Besides that, the agency must wholeheartedly believe in its own knowledge and expertise, and must demonstrate that belief by the sincerity with which it presents recommendations to its client. Such demonstration requires tact, diplomacy, and knowledge of human nature. If you plunge ahead blindly and insist that the client do something your way just because you say so, you can quickly lose the business. Remember always that you are dealing with areas of knowledge in which much uncertainty exists, proofs are difficult, and results stem from multiple causes. If, however, your attitude clearly shows that the betterment of the client's business is your sole purpose, at least you will be talking his or her own language. This factor alone should put you in a position in which your promotional advice is carefully considered.

Contrast this with the attitude of most young agencies: their primary end is to please the client. They make their plans and they write their copy in the hope of receiving the client's approval. Such agencies are unwittingly proceeding on the assumption that the client knows more about advertising than they do, which completely wipes out the reason for the agency's existence, apart from its mechanical functions.

Of course, we all know why so many agencies occupy this nonprofessional and subservient position in the economic scheme. Primarily it is because the results of advertising are so far removed from its creation and are further confused by the impact of other forces. So a client, concerned with the practical problems of sales and experienced in promotion, may well feel he or she knows as much or more about advertising than the agency. Occasionally he or she is right. So it is quite natural for the young agency to yield in such a situation, abandoning its birthright, if you please, and giving the client whatever he or she wants.

Taking the easiest way out, however, can be fatal to the agency. Sooner or later another agency will come along prepared to provide a more professional attitude and equipped to give the client services and direction the present agency has failed to offer. The account predictably changes hands.

One more important point about attitude. Agencies must recognize themselves for what they are—experts capable of using sound professional advice to improve the client's results—and that their service is an immensely valuable one for which they are entitled to adequate remuneration. Worthwhile advertisers will respect you more for demanding what you are worth, and unless you do, you are in for trouble.

So, by way of summary: for an agency to grow and prosper it must have a business philosophy combining both ability and attitude that demonstrates that it is capable of offering its clients sound business advice, that it is willing to rely on its own professionalism in doing so, and that it has the courage to charge what its advice is worth.

To Grow You Must First Survive

In spite of the difficulty of operating in an era of increasing costs, small agencies are continually being born, keep on operating, and grow steadily to a point where they provide a decent living for their people.

These successful agencies seem to conform to a common pattern. Externally, in the agency's relations with the outside world, it is a three-part pattern consisting of selling, planning, and performing; internally, within the agency's own management, the pattern is good housekeeping combined with proper human relations. Let's look at each of these five features in turn.

Selling

Smart small agencies find advertisers who need them. They make contact with these potential clients by letter, by telephone, by the Internet, and then later with personal meetings. They land a reasonable percentage of these prospects because they have what the advertiser needs, and they have developed ways of proving this in each case.

Planning

Once the account is in the shop (and often even earlier, while the solicitation is proceeding), these good small agencies formulate, visualize, and present carefully worked-out programs for increasing the client's sales, profits, and company reputation. Part of the agency's planning must concern itself with remuneration for its work and the division of labor between its staff and the client's sales staff, in what should be a joint effort to improve the client's business. No agency can do a good job for a client if it is not getting enough money for its work. Good planning includes complete listings of who does what and what the rate of pay is for doing it. Bad planning may later cause misunderstanding and irritation on either side of the desk.

Performance

Agencies promise plenty in advance, in their selling and in their planning; good agencies' performances exceed their promises. Well, shouldn't they, after all? Previously, an agency was on the outside looking in, handicapped by a lack of knowledge of the real difficulties confronting the advertiser. Now it is on the inside. It is a member of the client's family. In a well-organized relationship, nothing important is hidden from the agency. A good agency's staff brings wide experience and business judgment to bear upon problems that may have disconcerted an advertiser who has been up to his ears in them for years. New brains + new enthusiasm + new approaches = new results!

This personal attention, this identification of the client's welfare with that of the agency, is one of the cogent reasons for small agency success.

Good Housekeeping

This homey term best describes the successful internal management that marks the good small agency. Its financial affairs are sound. It gets paid what it deserves in a timely manner. It spends less than it takes in. It utilizes the resulting profit in three ways: as working capital, bonuses for the owners, and profit sharing for the employees.

Proper Human Relations

This is both an internal and an external attitude. The good agency behaves properly toward its clients and its suppliers. It is honest and decent in its dealings, reliable and careful with promises, and prodigal in performance. Also, the good agency is good to work for. It takes proper care of its people. It may pay them conservatively as it plays its finances very safe, but whatever profits there are it shares liberally. There is no feeling that the boss gets all the gravy or all the credit for ideas. Every person in the agency is happier working in that shop than he or she would be working for him- or herself.

How to Handle a Recessionary Period

The margin on which an ad agency operates is very slim. It takes very little reduction in income or increase in expenses to turn a profit into a loss. Also, because of its high visibility, the advertising budget frequently is one of the first items cut when the client begins to feel a financial pinch. So another vital part of the pattern for survival is the adoption of policies that will build bulwarks to protect the agency against temporary setbacks. The following three basic factors have helped agencies weather temporary reversals. They concern, as you see, money, people, and new business. They exemplify wise business judgment in how to cope not only with normal bad breaks but also with the particular hazards that characterize the agency business.

Cash Money

Agencies strong enough to weather bad times have built up their working capital steadily in years of prosperity instead of spending on larger quarters, unnecessary improvements, and too-generous profit sharing. It is a good rule to plow back a substantial part of profits into the business. If working capital has been small in relation to needs, many agencies have reinvested higher than normal percentages of their profits in good times, aiming at an eventual working capital figure large enough not only to handle all normal needs such as earning cash discounts and establishing excellent credit, but also to provide the extra margin of safety desirable for any business. A good rule of thumb is to build your working capital until it equals about one quarter of your total annual payroll. This will give you a cushion so you don't have to cut salaries and people at the first sign of a loss of billing, and thus throw overboard your most valuable asset—your people and their morale.

Multiple Ownership

The strongest agencies are those in which valuable people have been allowed to become part owners of the agency. Profit sharing is fine, but real ownership is better. Too many agencies, built up by the ability of the founder, strive to maintain benevolent autocracy.

A word of warning: in choosing people to participate in ownership, first be sure of the real value to the agency of the individuals concerned. Go slowly and surely, and give yourself an escape hatch in case the person concerned does not live up to expectations. A good partnership of two individuals should result in "one plus one equals more than two" in productivity.

Diversification of Accounts

In seeking new business, agencies should be wary of big accounts that may take all the agency's resources and abilities. The later loss of such business could cripple or wreck an agency. No one would be so foolish as to advise passing up a big account if you can get it, but at the same time be aware of the dangers inherent in dependence upon income from a single source.

This happens all the time in the agency business. One account becomes the linchpin, supports the agency, dominates the billing, and creates fear and trepidation that "if something happens to this account, we're all in big trouble."

One of our agency clients had an airline account that provided 60 percent of the agency's billing. The client went belly-up and left the agency in a very bad fix. It did recover, but it took a lot of wheeling and dealing with suppliers and the media before the agency was able to snap back.

The obvious answer, of course, is to maintain your new business efforts and attempt to balance out the various accounts so that one client doesn't overwhelm you. Total domination by the "big one" can use up your staff and cause the neglect of your other accounts as well as your new business development efforts. Here's a guideline to follow if you can: *Don't let one account represent more than 20 percent of your total billings.* Go after many small accounts; you can charge nominal service fees, which will help increase your income. Don't lose money on any one of them. Take bread and butter accounts, and industrial accounts. They're less glamorous, perhaps, but they appreciate the attention other agencies have denied them and can become safe, steady sources of income. Diversify. This policy has helped many an agency survive difficult times.

So, Having Survived, How About Growth?

By far your best source of new business is your present list of clients. Why? Well, in the first place, because you know them and they know you; they have confidence in you (or they'd be your ex-clients); and you're helping them grow and as they continue to grow so will you. But, you can't just sit back and take this relationship for granted; you must keep continually reminding the client how valuable you are to him or her. Here are some specific things you should do.

First, do outstandingly good, creative work. By that I mean new and advanced marketing ideas expressed in excellent copy, ingenious and effective media placement, and constant cooperation with the sales department of the advertiser.

Second, rub the advertiser's nose in this good work, tactfully and persuasively. If you don't tell him, and if possible prove to him, how good and effective the advertising is, he may not realize it. He doesn't know about advertising. How do you expect him to appreciate it unless you constantly sell it to him and the sales force?

Third, make the advertiser realize how much he is getting for his money. Contact reports help in this, but examples of money saving, space or time bought on better terms, production costs held down by skillful repetition of advertisements, and competitive prices from vendors—all these the agency should forcefully call to the advertiser's attention. It isn't enough to do an able job in landing his account, you have to keep on selling your value as long as that account is in the shop.

Fourth, remember that ours is a personal service business. The more you can keep all your client contacts on a highly personal and friendly basis, the more you can identify yourself with his or her business, the better off you will be. The small agency principals can afford to give more time to individual clients. They have time to worry, which is important. This situation accounts for the many agency-client relationships that are so long lasting, and that are usually terminated only by change in the personnel of the agency or the advertiser.

Fifth, although you may not be able to afford extra departments and services, you must offer them and make it constantly clear that whatever the advertiser could get from larger agencies he can get from you. It may be necessary to buy such services on the outside; however, the client needs to be told they are available. Remember, other agencies are constantly telling him how much he is missing.

Always remember that, in spite of whatever is done to get better and bigger, there will be a normal mortality rate among accounts, through no fault of yours. This attrition must be provided for in advance by constantly gunning for new business, in part to replace what will be lost, in part to continue growing.

No agency stands still. It either gains or loses; like a plant or flower, it either grows or dies. The agency that appears to be running along on an even keel with about the same billing every year is actually losing ground. Time is running out on it. The longer it holds on to an account, doing much the same thing year after year, the more the advertiser wonders if he couldn't possibly do better elsewhere. Sadly enough, our vulnerability increases with length of service. The national average for retaining an account is four-and-a-half years.

Every business has its good and its bad points. Ours is a remunerative, exciting, rewarding occupation. It is also highly unstable, subject to personal whims and vagaries, and little understood by the person who pays our bills.

You've got to be fast on your feet, sensitive to unexpected developments, able to spot trouble a mile off, and always conscious of the advertiser's attitude toward you before he senses it himself.

Yes, get better and get bigger as fast as is economically practicable. But most of all, get smarter. Learn how to think two jumps ahead of the client. Don't follow, lead. You're supposed to know more about promoting sales than he or she does; show that you do.

We tend to blame our losses of business on the larger size of other agencies, or on their offering something we cannot afford or should not offer. But are these the real reasons why another shop landed the business? We don't retain clients by being as good as our competitors; we hold them only by being better, constantly proving it, and telling the client about it. Basically, advertisers don't want to change agencies, in spite of their inherent restlessness. They know how much time will be required to educate the new agency. They'd like to stay, if we prove to them that staying with our agency is in their best interest.

— 2 —

A Look at Financial Reality

Vince Lombardi, the legendary football coach of the Green Bay Packers, always started out his first day of practice by displaying a football to the players. His opening remark was, "This is a football!" He then proceeded with the basics of how to play football and how to be a winning team.

Most agencies and studios are creative, know their marketing, handle clients professionally, and go after new business. Then why is it that four out of five of these firms are history at the end of five years? The successful ones (the one out of five that survives and prospers) *know how to manage their money.* The tradition has been that media will pay agencies 15 percent of the advertising space or time. The agency then bills the client 100 percent of the cost and pays the media 85 percent.

So, Let's Start with the Basics

Let's say that your agency has a gross billing (your total number of dollars that you bring in) of $1 million. After you pay direct costs, i.e., media placement, outside photography, printing, etc., you are left with *gross income* or *gross profit.*

Here is the basic lesson: *This is the only money you have to manage your business.*

If you spend too much for payroll, or rent, or other overhead expenses, you will lose money. It's that simple, it's that obvious, and it's also that difficult! If you control your costs, you will make a profit . . . guaranteed!

SOME PITFALLS TO AVOID

What pitfalls must many agency people, particularly those who are contemplating forming their own agencies, avoid? What causes agencies to fail?

When considering what you must watch out for—the hazards that can wreck even the best planned agency—you must always bear in mind the narrow margin on which the agency business operates. Based on figures from the American Association of Advertising Agencies, as published in *Advertising Age* from time to time, out of every dollar billed to the client, the agency immediately paid out to the media and suppliers slightly more than 79 cents, leaving barely 20 cents to meet all its own expenses and earn a profit. Less than 1 cent of gross billing remains as net profit. Here are the figures:

	Client Dollars	*Agency Percentages*
Billed to Clients	$100.00	
Paid to Media and Suppliers	79.56	
Retained by Agency	20.44	100.00%
Agency's Expenses	19.34	94.60
Profit Before Taxes	1.10	5.40
Income Taxes	0.27	1.34
Net Profit	0.83	4.06

Runaway Expenses

The first pitfall is failure to watch expenses like a hawk. These figures show that an expenditure of $11 for a client lunch must generate an additional $1,000 of billing or profit will suffer. Pretty scary, isn't it?

Employee Attitudes

A closely related pitfall is the failure to impress all your employees, and especially the account executives, that while they are working on the *client's* account, they are working for the *agency*. Never let them forget that their paychecks come from the agency and not from the client.

Of course, the agency and all its people must do the best job they can for the client, but they must exercise good business judgment when doing so. All too often this is interpreted as giving the client everything he or she could possibly want, such as four or five versions of every layout or the regular acceptance of rush jobs entailing overtime work. True, these all have to be done at times, but the agency man or woman who is thinking of the agency's (and his or her own) welfare, as well as the client's wishes, will insist on billing the client for the extras involved. He or she will probably be surprised to learn that, if properly approached with logical reasoning, the client is a reasonable person, too. There will be times when you have to give away services like these, but if your people understand and apply good business practices, at least you'll know what you're giving away and why.

Lack of Planning

By its very nature, an agency is highly dependent on the talents of a small group of people—and in its early stages, on the talents of one individual. So a prolonged illness or death can play havoc with an agency that hasn't foreseen these possibilities and made some advance provisions to meet them. Various kinds of insurance can help here, as well as plans for the succession of responsibilities in both the management of the agency and the handling of client contacts. Being involved in advertising networks and trade associations will keep you apprised of what one-person shops might be contracted to fill a temporary void.

Poor Management

Generally this arises because of the nature of the typical advertising person: creative, imaginative, impulsive, and outgoing, but often without knowledge of finance. He works hard, does a grand creative and marketing job, gives more service than he can possibly afford, and comes to the end of the year with a loss instead of a profit and the inescapable question, "How long can I stand this drain?" So, our agency principal must either acquire a sense for sound financial management or hire someone to manage the agency's finances. Most simply defined, this means spending less than you take in, thus showing a profit.

Profit can be increased in only two ways—either by reducing expenses or by increasing income. To maintain such a policy day in and day out requires courage on the part of the agency principal— the courage to say no to many requests for increased salaries or other expenditures and the courage to ask clients for more income in the form of fees or other charges when expenses cannot be cut further.

Go Easy on Extending Credit

Except in a few cases, like advertising for political candidates, advertising is placed on credit, not paid in cash. How far should an agency go in extending credit?

The imprudent extension of credit is undoubtedly the biggest pitfall of all. The peculiar economics of the agency business, with the agency working for the advertiser and yet being paid by the media through commissions, has its origins in the very early days when agencies were primarily brokers who bought space in wholesale quantities and resold it to their clients. Somewhere along the line they began to write copy to fill the space they had bought and the agency creative function was born. In those days, the media were dealing only with the agencies and obviously looked to them for payment for the space they bought. This is still a fundamental principle of the normal agency-media relationship and the contract form most commonly used states that, "Publisher agrees to hold Agency solely liable for payment."

In the aftermath of the Lennen & Newell and U.S. Media International failures, there was a trend to back away from agency sole liability, particularly on the part of the networks. In 1974, two networks sued advertisers for unpaid bills, but in 1977 the courts ruled against the networks, thus upholding the principle of sole agency responsibility for payment to media. This action apparently did not finally resolve the issue because CBS and Stokely-Van Camp reached an out-of-court settlement under which Stokely paid CBS a reputed $50,000 to save the cost of fighting the appeal that CBS had just filed. So, the question is still open as to how much liability falls on the advertiser.

Some agencies are including in their contract forms a limited liability clause; a typical one states "Agency shall pay for . . . broadcasts carried by Station . . . only if it first receives payment . . . from its client." Whether or not this would hold up in court no one knows.

In any event, the whole question of agency liability for media payments is very much up in the air, particularly since a lot of broadcast advertising is run without any formal signed contract at all. So until the situation has been cleared up by the courts, the prudent agency principal had better assume that he is going to be held liable for payment to media. This means that his neck is on the line and he must use due care in extending credit to his clients.

To avoid this dilemma, it is preferable not to extend credit at all. Set your billing dates and terms of payment so that you get your money before you're required to pay it out. Since this is contrary to the way most agencies operate, many feel that clients will resist the realistic request for payment before the agency is holding the bag. Not so! When the situation is properly presented, most honest clients see the reasonableness of the request, and think more highly of the agency that pursues this policy.

Another way to protect yourself is to be sure you collect your media dollars before the closing date. In the event the client hasn't paid you before the deadline, you can cancel the ad. For example, if you are placing a full-page ad in a trade journal with a thirty-day closing date, and if the ad is scheduled to run in November, then use this schedule as a guide:

September	*October*	*November*
Prepare insertion order for November insertion.	October 1 is the closing date. Make sure you receive your money by this date. If you don't, you can still cancel the ad.	Date of issue: if payment is made, ad runs.

But—and this is very important—put your method and timing of billing in writing and discuss it frankly with the client as early in your relationship as possible. Also, be sure at this point to get the client's financial personnel in on the act. They'll know what you're talking about and see the reasonableness of your arguments. Point out that, if they don't pay promptly, you're putting $79 of your own on the line in the expectation of keeping 83 cents. They'll get the idea!

There are two more ways to avoid becoming your clients' creditor. First, have the media bill the client the gross amount. When the media receives payment, the media will pay you your commission. Or, second, you can have the client pay the net amount to the media and issue your commission check directly to you.

Another point. Watch your receivables as though your life depended on it—for your corporate life may. Start to scream bloody murder the minute a bill becomes overdue. There's no surer recipe for the bankruptcy of an agency than to pay media for space or time you ordered and then have your client renege on paying you. By all means look into credit insurance; it can be expensive, particularly for less than top-rated clients, but it just may save your agency.

One last thought on the subject of credit. This is the matter of recognition that is granted by individual media or in many cases by such organizations as Media Credit Association (MCA) acting on behalf of many media. Recognition is simply a certification, based on an examination of your financial statements, that you seem to be financially reliable and can be expected to discount your bills. New statements are requested every six months or year to keep up to date. Formerly an agency without recognition was denied the 15 percent commission, which is paid by the media, but the only penalty today is a denial of credit and a requirement to pay cash with your order.

Just as the media keep an eye constantly on the agency through the recognition procedure, so the agency should keep an eye on its clients' financial health.

Subscribe to a regular financial reporting service such as Dun & Bradstreet. Don't take the attitude that this implies any distrust of your clients. It's just good business practice when you may be extending to a single client over the course of a year credit in an amount that exceeds your total working capital. If you can't afford Dun & Bradstreet, ask your own bank or a banking client to check the credit of new, unknown accounts.

DON'T FINANCE YOUR CLIENTS

Should an agency finance its clients? What does this really mean? What's so bad about it?

It always has been considered one of the cardinal principles of the agency business that the agency is expected to finance its own operations but not the advertising of its clients.

The first part of this statement simply means that the principals of an agency should be good enough businesspeople to operate at a profit and thus avoid dissipating the agency's resources simply to stay afloat. It also means that the agency will have started with (or built up over the years with retained profits) enough capital to see it through the ordinary ups and downs of business.

This is not to say that an agency's own resources must be enough to meet any contingency, but that its past performance plus current resources should be enough so that it can get needed financing from regular commercial sources to tide it over an unusually severe short-term financial bind. The key phrase here is "commercial sources." Avoid like the plague seeking financial help from clients! It's just bad business.

Let's look now at agency financing of clients. This is usually more subtle and occurs whenever the agency extends longer than normal credit to the client. The case where an agency simply lets its client's bills run along unpaid has been discussed in the preceding section. A more common form of client financing arises from the way agencies handle payment for production costs.

Some jobs—particularly large catalogs and similar pieces— are in process for several weeks or even months before they are completed. As each particular supplier involved in the job finishes its work it will send in a bill and the well-managed agency will pay it within its terms. If, however, the agency's billing arrangements with its clients call for billing production only when the job has been completed, it cannot immediately rebill to the client the amount it has paid out to the supplier, but must put it into a suspense account called "inventory" or "work in process" or some similar term. To the extent that such an account remains on the books, it constitutes financing the client's advertising. There are ways to get around this; they'll be covered in Chapter 9, "Billing for Your Services."

The ultimate example of financing the client occurs when the client has owed the agency money for a long time and professes inability to pay in cash, but offers his company's stock instead. Don't even think twice about it; utter a resounding "No!" Chances are, you'd probably lose your shirt, or at least a good part of it, and at best would be stuck with a frozen asset of questionable value.

If you have to accept something other than cash for your bills, get an interest-bearing note with a fixed maturity. If you have to, you can probably discount this at the bank. A corollary benefit of doing this is that in some cases, merely asking for a promissory note has resulted in payment of the debt in full, in cash.

This is not to say that you should never own a client's stock. The situation just described should not be confused with the situation in which an agency desires voluntarily to invest in its client's business, believing that its inside track puts it in a position to make a desirable profit by getting in on the ground floor of an opportunity not yet spotted by other investors. That's the way many advertising pioneers became rich.

So why shouldn't an agency finance a client?

Basically because an agency is not in the financing business (that's what banks are for); it has no skills in providing financing nor the investigatory facilities to tell a good financing deal from a bad one; and it has no mechanism set up to handle the details involved in financing. You're much better off providing good advertising and doing what you know best.

BEWARE OF CUT-RATING
AND REBATING

Another common problem is that many agencies practice a kick-back system in secret. Should you plan to swap punches with them *sub rosa?* Should you admit the situation and compete openly on a price basis?

Unfortunately, in today's competitive market hard negotiating with the media has become more prevalent. Many agencies will ignore the rate cards and start off by demanding the lowest cost per spot, which is obviously good for the client. In many cases, the stations will throw in "bonus spots" to entice the agency to make the buy. Bonus spots are extra spots that the station will run at no extra cost, usually in nonprime time.

So, if you're able to get a better rate for your client, you will be doing the client a real service. However, once you start the rebating game, it eventually leads to further problems. Rebating is simply a "kickback" with cash or credit given to the client, as opposed to cut-rating, which passes on the savings to the client.

Don't for a minute forget that the only things you or any agency have to sell are the time and talents of yourself and your associates. If you regularly give them away below their real worth, clients and prospective clients can't be blamed for accepting your evaluation. And you'll have trouble generating enough income to stay in business, let alone grow and prosper. Have the courage of your convictions and charge what your services are worth. The client will respect you for it.

While there is nothing wrong about an agency cutting prices to get new business, these questions pose another aspect of the problem: Does it work? It often gets business. But then what?

All too frequently an agency that gets a piece of new business by price cutting gives the impression that this is its normal operating procedure, and the client comes to expect all future work to be on the same low-cost basis. Agency service, for the best interests of the advertiser, consists of hard thinking and planning to increase the client's sales, reputation, and profits. This means time spent by the agency heads and the top talent, not the clerical force or any other of the mechanical elements of the agency operation. An agency simply cannot afford to use this expensive talent to the extent it should unless it is liberally paid for it. With competition what it is, nothing but the best has a chance to be seen and to be effective. The best costs money. If large portions of an agency's business are regularly handled on the basis of price concessions, it cannot hope to survive and increase, to make a profit year after year, to grow in strength and reputation. Clients need to see that keeping the agency healthy will ensure that the clients continue to reap the benefits of the agency's talents and knowledge of their business. Insisting on cost cutting now may mean that the clients will have to spend a lot of time and money breaking in a new agency when they have forced their current one out of business.

Just as an agency can't grow and prosper by regularly undercharging for its services, neither can it do so by regularly overcharging the client and making inordinate profits. Mutually agreeable terms, reviewed by both parties at frequent intervals to reflect changing conditions, will ensure the futures of both client and agency.

To Spec or Not to Spec

At an agency network meeting, the speakers asked the agency participants, "How many of you believe in doing speculative presentations?" Only one person raised her hand. Speculative presentations—known as "specs"—require an agency to do all the work it would for a paying client, but with no guarantee of payment. The agency is paid only if the client likes the work enough to hire it.

The speakers then asked, "How many agencies here do spec work to get new clients?" About half of the participants admitted that they do speculative presentations. None of them wanted to, but all felt that sometimes it was necessary!

As in previous examples where a client may wish to see five versions of an ad but only wants to pay for the one used, specs can be a fast track to insolvency.

There are no hard-and-fast rules as to whether one should do spec work. It depends upon the agency's philosophy, its approach to new business, how hungry it is, and how much of a risk it wants to take. Full-blown dog-and-pony shows can be very costly in terms of production expense as well as in the hours the staff spends on them. They also can be the way to land a new, big account. (No agency will do spec work without hope of a *large* reward.)

Don't Spend Money

- Never prepare a spec presentation when you don't know the product, its distribution situation, or the philosophy of the prospect.
- Don't ever do a surprise spec proposal. When unsolicited presentations are made, agencies are usually so far off the target, they don't have a chance.
- Don't make a spec presentation if you don't have the final decision maker involved in the process. It too often happens that a subordinate will ask for a presentation but doesn't have the power to make a decision. Final decision goes upstairs to someone who hasn't seen the pitch.

Maybe Spend Money

Depending on your plan for growth, you *might* consider a spec presentation

- when the client will pay for your expenses, or for all, or part, of the costs involved.

- when the prospect makes a request for a presentation without your solicitation. This prospect has some positive thoughts about your shop or he wouldn't have come to you. When the prospect approaches you, he or she is willing to spend a lot of valuable time getting you on the right track.

- when you have all the marketing facts, and then the prospect shares everything with you. That's a pretty good sign that he or she means business.

— 3 —

How to Start Your Own Agency

This valuable advice is from Professor Theodore Beckman of Ohio State University: "If you want to go into the agency business for yourself, you must go to work for another agency, and get the bruises, the problems, the experience at their expense. After you've been totally involved in acquiring and handling clients, and understand the finances of running an agency, then you might be ready to go out on your own." This has proven to be so important for countless agency owners.

In so many instances, media representatives (salespeople), printers, and all those others who have worked *with* advertising agencies, decide to go into the agency business and pick up an easy 15 percent agency commission from selling advertising space. They have no idea what's involved with preparing and presenting a total marketing plan, as well as understanding there's more to it than just placing a media schedule.

SHOULD YOU START YOUR OWN AGENCY?

Hope must indeed still spring eternal and the entrepreneurial urge run strong judging by the number of inquiries I've had about going into the agency business.

Some optimists think it looks like an easy way to make money and just want to be told how to go about it. Other better qualified businesspeople, with genuine reasons for starting their own shops, ask to have their figures checked out. Here are a few observations that may be useful.

First of all, remember that most people who plan on going into the agency business underestimate their expenses and overestimate their income, so it is wise to allow a large margin of error to compensate for this natural human attitude. Be conservative in your original planning to avoid rude shocks later on.

An advertising agency is an expensive operation, involving a place in which to work, furniture, fixtures, supplies, and equipment. A number of people must be hired or their services contracted, according to the volume of business you plan to handle at the outset.

These expenses will be of two sorts, initial (nonrecurring) and continuous (operating). The funds to meet initial expenses must come from the original capital advanced by the founders.

Once the agency is set up and ready for business, the question becomes "Where is the money coming from for operating expenses, and how soon?" The second part of this question is important. There is a lag, often of many weeks, between the time an agency incurs a financial obligation or actually has to pay out money, and the time when cash is received from the client.

The first thing to look at, then, is gross income for the agency. This means the money the agency retains after paying media and suppliers and which it uses to pay expenses. To the greatest possible degree, this gross income must be sure. It must be adequate. Lacking either of these characteristics, you are headed for trouble.

Therefore, start out by investigating the realistic expectation of continuing income. This is not easy because, even if you have written assurances from clients based on their advertising plans, there is nothing to prevent these plans from being changed or delayed. If you can get a contract guaranteeing retainer fees you are better off, but this may be hard for a new agency.

Not only must you get business in order to run an agency—you must make sure you will be able to hold on to it. Most contracts give you only ninety days protection. Theoretically your entire business, and the income derived from it, can fly out the window within this time. To retain advertising or promotional billings, you must continuously deliver satisfactory service. That, in turn, depends entirely on people—yourself and your associates.

So there is a clear element of risk involved in the question of income to the agency. It is difficult to figure this risk correctly; however, your success or failure may rest squarely on how you solve this problem.

So, having assured a continuing income, as best you can, the question becomes "How much income is necessary?" All the current figures show that income should be at least 20 percent of billing—so an agency billing a nice round $5 million should try to get gross income of $1 million, at the least. Since media commissions are at a fixed rate of 15 percent of billing, the difference will have to come from markups on outside purchases, charges for copy, art, etc., done by your own people and, quite likely, fees of one sort or another. You must be prepared to draw up a schedule of charges for these services. It must be competitive in your market; it must be one you can justify to clients; and, above all, it must produce the income you need to reach your $1 million.

You also must be prepared to operate initially at a loss. Even if you budget your expenses so they will absorb only $900 thousand of your $1 million on a regular basis, and thus give you a 10 percent profit, you initially will be in the red for quite a while: This results from the lag between the time the idea is born, the client is billed, and you are paid. A reasonable allowance for this is three months.

So, an agency just starting business will begin incurring expenses for salaries, rent, etc., the day it opens its doors, but will not receive any appreciable income (except from fees) for about three months. In this period it will have spent one quarter of its annual expense budget or, using our sample figures, $225 thousand. It would be in the red by the difference between that figure and the incidental income and fees received. Obviously, it is going to take a while to start showing a profit.

This points up another factor the new agency head must consider: the necessity of providing enough capital to buy needed furniture, computers, fax machines, supplies, etc., and to cover operating expenses until income starts coming in. A good rule of thumb for an agency of the size described here would be $250 thousand or 25 percent of our stated anticipated annual gross income. If you can't put up that much yourself, or borrow it, you can consider offering part ownership to some of the key people who will be working with you, but don't do this unless you know them and their abilities thoroughly. Above all, during your starting days don't allow any outsider to make even a small investment of cash in your enterprise just to build up your working capital. When you do this, you are selling part of your business before you know what it is worth and before you know as much as you should about the person involved. This, I find, is a mistake made frequently by people new to the agency business. It can be embarrassing and expensive.

Once the new agency is assured of income and of its continuance, the next requirement for success would seem to be knowing where you are financially at all times. How you are doing, month by month. This, of course, calls for experienced financial management.

You will best allocate this job to someone else, since it is difficult, specialized work and you are likely to need all your time running your shop and keeping both your clients and your employees happy. You will need an accurate cost system, administered by an expert. Don't economize on this. It can make or break you. You must be apprised steadily of whether you are running ahead or behind, where you are making money, and where you are losing it. Given this information, you must act fast and with courage, allowing yourself to be influenced as little as possible by emotion.

Finally, I would suggest as an essential of success in today's business that you sense your client's needs before he does. Don't sit back comfortably assuming that everything is all right just because the relationship is continuing and nobody seems to be complaining. Your security is constantly being undermined by the client's normal dissatisfaction with everything except his own performance, and by claims set up by competing agencies. I strongly believe that the future of the entire agency business, and getting proper payment for their work, depends upon the extent to which agencies render valuable business advice.

So, by way of summary and with a note of encouragement, you've set up an agency, assured a reasonable and continuing income, and weathered the first rough months. Now, how do you earn a profit, and having earned it, what do you do with it?

You turn a profit in managing an agency by first setting the profit aside, then running the business by spending only what's left over. It's like managing a household budget by putting a series of coffee cans labeled "groceries," "clothes," "rent," "insurance," etc., on a shelf. At the beginning of each month, you divide up the money for running the household and put the proper amount in each of the coffee cans. When a payment is to be made, you take the money out of the appropriate can—but never out of the neighboring one.

In your case, as agency manager, one of your cans is labeled "profit." (In actual practice this "can" might be a special bank account.) Whenever a dollar of gross income is received, you immediately take 20 cents of it (or whatever amount represents your planned profit) and put it in the profit can. Only after you've done this do you divide the remainder of the gross income among the other cans that represent different kinds of operating expenses. Like the household manager who scrupulously respects the can labels, never take anything out of the profit can until the end of the year. Then you divide up the contents between bonuses, profit sharing, additions to working capital, etc.—all, of course, according to plan.

You show a profit from an advertising agency only if you decide to operate so a profit is assured, which means sacrifice and rigid economy. Some people are content to operate only for their own pay and that of those associated with them, in the hope of future growth. This is unwise. Insisting on a profit is more than a theoretical desirability; it makes for financial soundness and assures capital growth. It definitely bears on the agency's credit position.

In the early days of the agency you may feel that paying part of your profits to your employees in the form of profit sharing is premature, in which event you split your profits between yourself and your business in whatever proportions seem best. However, the sooner your associates begin sharing in the shop's profits, the sounder your personnel relations will be.

SHOULD YOU BUY AN AGENCY?

Instead of going through the problems of starting a new agency, wouldn't it be better to buy one already operating? If so, what should you look out for? On its face this seems like a good idea—if you are buying what you think you are, if the values are really there, and if the price is right. For the moment let's forget about price, which is covered in the valuation section of Chapter 11, and talk about what you're buying.

You're Buying Net Assets

This is pretty simple and the main thing to check out is that the assets are real and not imaginary, and that all offsetting liabilities, both present and contingent, are disclosed. Accounts receivable from clients are usually one of the largest assets and one of the hardest to evaluate properly. They should be examined critically to see if there are substantial amounts that are in dispute or badly in arrears—and adjustments made accordingly. All of this is the kind of thing any competent accountant with some knowledge of agencies can evaluate and you certainly should hire one to do so.

You're Buying Future Earning Power

This has been called "going business value" or "goodwill," but, in its simplest terms, you are buying a source of future income and the facilities to handle that income and convert it into continuing profits. There are several major components of this future earning power.

Clients. The continuing loyalty of clients is the lifeblood of the agency business. Have the important clients been taken into anybody's confidence and told about the impending sale of the agency? Or have they just been left in the dark for fear that consulting them might rock the boat? "Rock" is a mild term for it when they are offered, as a *fait accompli,* a brand new agency picture they may or may not like.

Barring actual guarantees of continuance by responsible clients, account shifts are more likely than not, especially when new agency personnel are involved. New ownership gives the client firm an "out" if it has been looking for one. Its obligations to past ownership are now discharged. It fears a change of agency policy, so "it's a good time to be looking around to see if we can buy anything better, or for less money." A very dangerous time, indeed.

People. When you buy a conjectural future earning power, you must pay particular attention to the factors that will affect account retention. Possibly the most important of these is the personality of the agency owner and the account representatives who have been contacting and handling the business. Accounts stay with agencies, and correspondingly leave them, on a personal basis more often than is generally realized. We like to think accounts stay with us because of the good job we do for them; frequently, however, what holds them is the client's relationship with the account executive.

So, buying an agency in which the previous owner and/or his key people stay on the job is a very different proposition from buying one where they disappear from the picture. Good as the new owners may be, they are likely to be disagreeably disappointed by the way some business departs with their predecessors. So, assure yourself as much as possible of the continuing participation of the key people from the old regime. If those people are going to leave, make sure your sales contract precludes them from setting up a new shop and taking their current clients with them. You may want to look at current employees' contracts to see if they contain such a clause and if the clause is still enforceable if the agency is sold.

Deals. A stable list of clients is very important. But, behind that stability, are they all what they seem to be? Are there any special deals of one sort or another that would tend to make future income less than you'd expect? Better check them out!

Reputation. When you take over as new owner you'll find your road a lot smoother if you have the support and backing of the local media, suppliers, banks, civic organizations, etc. It'll be a lot easier to get and keep this support if the agency you're taking over has a good reputation in town. Check it out. Tell these groups of your plans and enlist their support. It should be easy to get if you start from a good base.

So, having determined what you're buying, it's wise to stop a minute and look with a jaundiced eye at why the agency is for sale. If it's as sound and profitable as it appears, why does the present owner want out? Maybe he is just getting tired of the rat race and wants to take things easy; maybe family health dictates a better climate; or just maybe (how cynical can you get?) he knows something and is trying to unload a potential lemon. Take a while to look into this gift horse's mouth—it may save you a bundle of bucks.

Provide an escape hatch in case things really go sour. Of course, if an agreement has been entered into in good faith, the honorable purchaser will be bound by its terms even if the business falls apart completely. But the terms of payment or the basis for calculating the final total price can be so drawn as to provide some relief in case of a serious reversal. It's far better to think of all the bad things that can happen and try to provide for them in advance, in a calm and reasoned way, than to try to devise emergency measures in the midst of a crisis.

— 4 —

You Can Help Build
Consumer Believability

Unfortunately, many surveys indicate that a large percentage of the population does not believe advertising claims. You can really help make a difference!

Advertising can take many forms—one woman telling another about a product she likes (word of mouth, the best there is); a million dollars' worth of time and talent seen on a nationwide television network; a card saying "good for colds" on your druggist's counter; a postcard from your car dealer; a turtle with "Souvenir of Miami" painted on its shell; a four-color gatefold in a national magazine; the smell of popcorn wafting from a store; or an enticing, easy-to-find Web page. All these are advertising, and if you try to say what they have in common you will come up with two correct conclusions: they are all forms of communication and they all aim to convince someone of something.

It has been said frequently that the aim of advertising is the sale. This, however, is true only in some cases. Such forms of advertising as mail order and direct mail aim almost solely to complete the sale. By far the greatest volume of advertising, however, aims at conviction only—the establishment of a favorable frame of mind—so that when the demand and the supply source come together, the sale results.

Advertising prepares the ground. It informs and convinces the consumer that a product or service is desirable and then that a specific product or service fits that desirable image.

This situation is true of the majority of products and services we use and of general ideas we entertain. For almost everything, there is in our minds a picture or an image, concerning which we subconsciously feel: "This is what it should be."

An agency's main reason for existence is its ability to give good promotional advice. It offers experienced business judgment in the narrow and specialized field of selling. Once this good sense is utilized by the client for plans and strategies, it is further implemented by all the agency's copy and art talent, all its marketing know-how, and all its experience in buying space, time, and materials. It is most important for us to recognize this sequence, this double importance of plan and performance. Good strategy and smart execution are as good a formula as you are likely to encounter for advertising success.

Once you recognize the importance of this preliminary thinking—business judgment projected into the future—you see more clearly how important it is that the agency be free to speak its mind, influenced only by the best interests of the client. Anything that interferes with this free thinking and free speaking does the client a disservice.

What kinds of restrictions are there on an agency's freedom? There are several, and unfortunately they seem to be increasing in number and severity.

FEAR OF THE CLIENT

More than most of us are willing to admit, our recommendations are influenced by fear of the client. We make plans based on what we think the customer will approve, rather than what we know is best. This bad basic situation must be resisted at all times. Once we allow this expediency to govern us, we lose all standing as independent advisers. We have bowed to a conflict of interest. We have put immediate profits first. Any client who has sense enough to make a success of his own business quickly sizes us up correctly, and begins to look around, like Diogenes, for an honest agency.

Another aspect of this can arise as a result of the way an agency is compensated. If compensation is based primarily on the commission method, there may be an unconscious predilection on the agency's part to recommend increased media expenditures since this increases agency income, or there may be some feeling by the client that this is what the agency is doing.

If, on the other hand, the agency is compensated by fees, it can make whatever recommendations it sincerely feels are best for the client without in any way affecting its own income. I know of several cases in which agencies, under these circumstances, have recommended a cessation of all advertising for a period. This is real freedom to give sound advice.

FALSE AND DECEPTIVE ADVERTISING

As we all know, there is a dangerous and rapidly widening gap between consumers and producers of goods and services. There is increasing public distrust, not only of advertising, but of all business. Why? Well, by its very nature, advertising always operates in the full glare of publicity. So the errors, exaggerations, and downright falsehoods of the few, the dishonorable—if not quite dishonest—claims, and the phony demonstrations are magnified and blown up by publicity, scandal, and the well-recognized human propensity to find bad things more interesting than good ones.

Does this unfavorable opinion of advertising do the business real harm? Of course it does. Each piece of deception, major or minor, increases the incredulity defensive minds raise against all selling endeavors. The more advertising indicates to people that it cannot be trusted, the more it costs advertisers to create belief. Heaven knows there is enough normal resistance without so stupidly increasing it!

Two attitudes characterize the buying frame of mind. One is a desire that the seller tell its story as favorably as possible, emphasizing its good points and minimizing its bad ones. So we find the buyer considering advertising a pleasing combination of all those devices the seller selects to please, attract attention, entertain, and create a favorable atmosphere. What a delightful prospect!

Alongside this friendly attitude, however, is another and sometimes even stronger attitude which may seem to be inconsistent. This is, "Don't fool me. You're signing your name to this story you're telling me. Lord help you if it isn't true!" Here is incipient resentment. And the more courteously the consumers have listened to your story, the madder they get when they find out they've been had.

The most hopeful element in the problem is the demonstrable fact that true, sincere, and informative advertising pays off, while false advertising falls flat on its face. So, regardless of restrictions imposed by outside sources, the pure economics of advertising dictate that the wise agency, in its own selfish interests, should put restrictions on its freedom of action. It should strive to produce only sincere, honest, and informative advertising.

Industry Self-Regulation

Another limitation on agency freedom is found in the advertising industry's own regulatory mechanism. This takes many different forms, some of them of long standing.

Individual Media

The earliest example of self-regulation was the establishment of standards by individual publishers or broadcasters. These usually have taken the form of an "advertising acceptability guide," but two prominent magazines, *Good Housekeeping* and *Parents,* have adopted seals of approval that they grant to advertisers whose products pass strict performance tests and meet their advertised claims. Since each of these sets of standards is different, you may find yourself with an advertisement that is acceptable to one medium, but not to another. A good example is the major oil company that had a commercial rejected as controversial by two television networks, yet accepted by the third.

Industry Groups

As early as 1924 the American Association of Advertising Agencies (AAAA) drew up a creative code setting forth standards of ethics and good taste in advertising. This code now has been endorsed by almost all major advertising and advertiser associations.

The first major effort to set up a mandatory code came in 1952 when the National Association of Broadcasters (NAB) drew up a code for both radio and television that set forth standards of good taste and acceptability for both commercials and program content.

In 1971 the National Advertising Review Board (NARB) was set up with the support of all sectors of the advertising industry. Its purpose is to deal effectively with deception and bad taste in national advertising. As an offshoot of this movement there has been a substantial revival of the Better Business Bureau movement and the establishment of local NARBS.

GOVERNMENT REGULATION

The first involvement by the government in the control of advertising came in 1872 with the passage of post office laws designed to curb the use of the mails to defraud. There is no exact count of federal government agencies that participate in regulating advertising, but the list keeps growing. Happily, occasionally one drops out of the regulatory picture, like the Federal Energy Administration, which during the OPEC oil crisis in the 1970s took it upon itself to forbid the oil companies' use of hard-sell tactics for their products. Other examples of government regulation are the required statement "use only as directed" in many television commercials for proprietary drug products and the complete ban on cigarette advertising on broadcast media that is now threatening to spread to all media.

CONSUMERISM AND SPECIAL INTEREST GROUPS

Self-designated consumer advocates are everywhere today and every major government agency has at least one on its staff. Add to these a large group of ivory-tower dwellers who seem to feel that every stream should flow with nothing less than distilled water and that the air we breathe should contain absolutely no particulates. Finally, add a liberal pinch of special-interest people who feel it is demeaning to show a woman as a homemaker or to show a minority group member working at a job at the lower end of the pay scale. Take all these people together and you have a small but very vocal minority who yell loudly enough so some political types are tempted to put unrealistic restrictions on advertising in order to "protect" consumers from perils of which they're not even aware, much less worried about.

To show what can happen, here is the problem encountered by an Ohio agency seeking to produce a television commercial for a nine-inch rubber ball. The description is in the words of the agency's Creative Director.

> It was decided to use tried and true techniques—like emulating *Sesame Street,* with lots of color, animation, and talking letters; use as voice-over a male talent who'd had a successful kids' TV show for years; use to represent the kids "The Singing Angels," a group of nationally known, well-adjusted, all-American youngsters. The commercial was written, the audio track cut, and the animation done. The material was sent to a well-known Chicago production house and all hell broke loose.
>
> The production house had sent the commercial out for network clearance and called to advise us to scrap everything and start over. Apparently a group of energetic crusading Boston mothers, self-designated ACT (Action for Children's Television), had gotten the ear of a federal regulatory body and NAB (National Association of Broadcasters) and the commercial was not approved.
>
> The first meeting with NAB showed just a few things wrong with the spot. *Sesame Street* and talking letters were forbidden; animation is not true life and hence *verboten;* no excitement, either visual or audio, was allowed; the time-tested television personality used off-camera "sounded like a drill instructor hoarse from shouting at the children" and did not represent a true play situation. It did not meet the criterion that commercials aimed at kids must show real-life scenes and activities as they would appear to the eyes of other kids.

Like it or not; until the pendulum swings back to a more realistic balance between reality and wild-eyed daydreaming over unattainable goals, you, as an agency person, are going to have to pay attention to these points of view and thus limit your freedom as how best to serve your clients.

In summary, there are restrictions on your freedom in advising your clients. Some of them are specific and must be complied with; others are subject to interpretation. In the long run, however, the best way to avoid running afoul of most restrictions is to produce good, honest, believable advertising that is in good taste. In the hard glare of publicity in which our industry operates, anything less is quickly evident and in the long run, self-defeating.

— Part II —

Agency Financial
Operations

— 5 —

Road Map for Your
Operating Figures

An advertising agency receives its income from three major sources:

1. Agency commission—a 15 percent standard commission given to recognized agencies for placing the advertising in various media. The commission is granted by the media. So the agency pays 85 percent of the media charge and bills the client 100 percent.

2. Retainer fees (service charge)—the agency agrees to handle all the phases of the advertising account providing agency service. The fee does not include outside expenses such as printing, photography, etc.

3. Markup—a percentage is added to outside production costs from vendors and then the total is billed to the client.

So many factors can affect the bottom line when running an agency. Trying to fit all agencies into a "standard mold" doesn't make sense; some agencies place a high percentage of billing on media that brings down the gross income to 15 percent (or lower if media is placed at less than 15 percent). Other agencies that charge high retainer fees or produce a lot of collateral materials with considerable creative fees and high mark-ups will, of course, show a high gross income. We have worked with agencies that show a gross income of more than

60 percent. The basic key to solvency and growth is still how you allocate your dollars within the gross income.

BASIC OPERATING FORMULA

No one can possibly run a business as highly personal and creative as an advertising agency by feeding standard percentages into a computer and letting it tell you how to spend your money. On the other hand, you can't be sure of running a successful operation if you completely ignore the accumulated experience of others and rely on luck and a fast infield to produce a profit at the end of the year.

Some target figures are a useful thing to have, as long as you recognize them merely as guidelines and not gospel, because spending less than you make, and thus showing a profit, is still the best definition of sound financial management. This is achieved either by holding down costs or by increasing revenue.

First, you must know how much you can expect to retain from each dollar you bill your clients to meet expenses and earn a profit. The following table gives the figures for a large number of agencies over a period of years. Look into this more closely because of two trends that exist. The first of these is that as agencies grow in size, the percentage of their billings converted into agency gross income declines. On the other hand, this percentage tends to rise as the years pass. Here are the figures:

		Gross Income as a Percentage of Billing		
Agency Size Group		*1972*	*1985*	*1995*
1	(Smallest)	21.73%	24.44%	28%
2		22.82	21.43	32
3		20.52	25.86	26
4		17.74	19.34	21
5		15.47	18.22	24
6	(Largest)	17.82	18.05	29
	All Groups	*20.72%*	*22.60%*	*26.99%*

Throughout this book, the basis on which almost all comparisons are made is the agency's gross income, so it is vital to know what your agency's gross income is or will be.

A second basic figure you must know in planning and controlling your operations is the number of employees needed to handle each $100 thousand of agency gross income. As you would expect, this figure becomes smaller as time passes and also as an agency grows. Here are the figures you can expect:

	Employees per $100,000 of Gross Income		
Agency Size Group	1972	1985	1995
1 (Smallest)	5.37	3.32	1.5
2	3.84	2.19	1.4
3	3.72	1.80	1.3
4	3.27	1.63	1.2
5	3.14	1.49	1.1
6 (Largest)	3.42	1.40	1.1
All Groups	*4.07*	*1.68*	*1.2*

Financial data for the last three years show that agencies on the average spent 53.6 percent of their gross income on payroll and related expenses and 34.6 percent on all other expenses, leaving a profit before taxes of 11.8 percent.

Experience with many agencies over a period of many years shows that a typical breakdown of an agency's total expenses would look like this:

Typical Breakdown of Agency Costs As Percentages of Gross Income

Payroll and Related Expense:
    Direct Payroll:

Client Contact	18.7%	
Creative	18.1	
Production	7.1	
Total Direct Payroll		43.9%

    Indirect Payroll:

General and Administrative	6.0	
Executive Overhead	4.5	
Total Indirect Payroll		10.5
Total Payroll and Related Expense:		54.4%

continued

Nonpayroll Expense:

Client Service Expense	5.0		
Space and Facilities Expense	12.1		
Corporate Expense	6.2		
Professional Fees/Employee			
Benefits/All Other	11.4		
Total Nonpayroll Expense		34.7	
Total Agency Expense			89.1%
Profit			10.9
			100.0%

Agency profit goals can vary widely, and for a great many perfectly good reasons, but sound agency budgeting requires first setting the amount of profit you want to shoot for and then controlling your expenses so you come up with that profit. This table is designed to help you do that:

Target Agency Expenses for Various Levels of Profit

Target Profit Level	5.00%	10.00%	15.00%	20.00%
Payroll and Related Expense	67.73%	64.16%	60.60%	57.03%
Nonpayroll Expense	27.27	25.84	24.40	22.97
Total Agency Expense	95.00%	90.00%	85.00%	80.00%
Profit Before Taxes	5.00%	10.00%	15.00%	20.00%

All these terms will be defined and described in detail later, but here it will suffice to point out that these are functional targets and the same employee may have chargeable time in several different categories. The more an owner pays herself for writing copy, the less she can pay a copywriter. What salaries you can pay to executives depends entirely upon what they do and how many hours they spend on each of their activities.

Now, for an example of how this formula works for controlling agency operations and profit, let's assume you want to earn a profit of 10 percent of income. This means that you must set aside this 10 percent first and spend only the remaining 90 percent. From the previous example, you'd expect this to be broken down to 64.16 percent for salaries and 25.84 percent for all other expenses but, obviously, you can shift expenses at will between categories as long as you don't run over the 90 percent total.

A well-conceived and carefully run cost system is, of course, an essential when you run an agency in this manner. The cost system must show accurately the cost of each function performed for each client if it is to be the principal tool for the control of operations and profit.

SIGNIFICANT RATIOS

Compiled here for ready reference is a list of the financial figures that are most significant and useful in controlling an agency's operations. Each is shown in the range in which you'd expect it to fall. Since every agency operates in a different way, these figures can only be considered as guidelines.

Guidelines for Expenses

Each of these expense guidelines is expressed as a percentage of total agency gross income.

	High	*Low*
Payroll and Related Expense:		
Direct Payroll:		
Client Contact	19.84%	16.71%
Creative	16.72	14.08
Production	11.66	9.82
Total Direct Payroll	48.22%	40.61%
Indirect Payroll:		
General and Administrative	8.57	7.21
Executive Overhead	10.94	9.21
	19.51%	16.42%
Total Payroll and Related Expense	67.73%	57.03%
Nonpayroll Expense:		
Client Service Expense	4.57%	3.85%
Space and Facilities Expense	15.13	12.75
Corporate Expense	5.83	4.91
Professional Fees	1.74	1.46
	27.27%	22.97%
Total Expense	*95.00%*	*80.00%*

Guidelines for Working Capital

The basic comparison for working capital is with total annual payroll. Other derived relationships are to gross income and billing.

	High	Low
Working Capital as a Percentage of Payroll	27.5%	22.5%
Working Capital as a Percentage of Income	16.5	13.5
Working Capital as a Percentage of Billing	3.5	2.5

Guidelines for Net Worth

The basic comparison for net worth is with gross income. From this is derived a relationship to billing.

	High	Low
Net Worth as a Percentage of Gross Income	35.0	25.0
Net Worth as a Percentage of Billing	7.0	5.0

LATEST INFORMATION FROM AAAA

- Out of 127 agencies reporting to AAAA with gross incomes between $1.5 million and $6 million, the average gross income is 31 percent. The smaller the shop, the larger the percentage.

- Gross income as a percentage of gross billing ranges from 14 to 40 percent.

- The average number of people required to handle each $100 thousand in gross income is .95 (about one person).

- Percentage of gross income for rent and facilities (leasing, depreciation, rent, space, and facilities) is 13 to 15 percent.

- Corporate expenses—new business, operating costs, dues, donations, etc.—range from 5 to 6 percent.

— 6 —

Billing, Income, and Profit

UNDERSTANDING THE TERMS

The advertising agency has its own set of terms that are alien to most other businesses. Our experience in working with bookkeepers and accountants is that they will relate expenses (payroll, rent, overhead) to sales instead of to gross income. Since (as we have mentioned several times, and bears repeating) you can only pay your expenses with the money that belongs to you, and not from billings, your overhead expenses can only be taken from gross income.

Are you confused by numbers that represent "billing" or "capitalized billing" or "gross income"? Does profit, when expressed both before and after taxes and as a "percentage of billing" or a "percentage of gross income," also present problems?

Billing

First, there is no real mystery about the simple term "billing" (or "sales," as it is sometimes called). This is simply the total of all the bills the agency sends to the client—bills for media at gross rates (that is, including commission), bills for advertising services and materials purchased from outside sources (including, of course, a markup or

47

agency service charge), bills for layout, copy, and other work done by your own staff, and finally, bills for any retainers or other fees.

Well, you ask, if this is such a simple concept, why doesn't everybody use it? There are two reasons. First, most of the dollars listed as billing pass right through the agency with hardly a pause. On media bills 85 percent is paid immediately to the media, and on production bills generally between 75 percent and 80 percent is immediately paid. None of this money can be used for the agency's own operations and hence it does not truly reflect the size of the agency as a business enterprise.

Second, some kinds of billing dollars are worth more than others as far as the agency's operations are concerned. Out of every media dollar the agency retains fifteen cents to help meet its expenses; out of the production dollar it keeps about twenty or twenty-five cents; out of the fee dollar it keeps one hundred cents. So, before you can use a billing figure to compare one agency with another, you have to know what makes up the billing of each of them.

Measuring Your Agency Size by "Capitalizing" Your Billing

It's surprising how many agency principals do not understand what *capitalized* billings are all about. Yet billings is the yardstick by which the size of an agency is most generally measured.

There is a completely ethical, legitimate way to increase that number and reflect a larger size for your shop. This is by *capitalizing* these gross income dollars. Capitalized billings is a standard measure for comparing the size of agencies. When you see the *Advertising Age* listing of agency billings, you may note that all billings are shown as capitalized billings.

So, what are capitalized billings? Very simply, when you see that number you know that gross income of the agency is 15 percent of the capitalized figure. Or looking at it from the other perspective, the gross income is capitalized upward to a figure that would produce a gross income that is 15 percent of the capitalized figure.

Here's how to capitalize your billing: Take your actual gross income and multiply it by 6.67. This gives you a number of which 15 percent is your gross income. Let's take the billing of two different agencies to demonstrate the procedure. (Numbers have been rounded off.)

Agency ABC		Agency XYZ	
Actual Billing	$1,000,000	Actual Billing	$1,000,000
Gross Income (15%)	150,000	Gross Income	300,000
Capitalized Billing:		Capitalized Billing:	
Multiply $150,000		Multiply $300,000	
by 6.67 and have		by 6.67 and have	
a capitalized		a capitalized	
billing of	$1,000,500	billing of	$2,001,000

What is the difference here? Agency ABC earned a gross income of $150 thousand on actual billings of $1 million while Agency XYZ earned $300,000 on the same billings. Therefore, XYZ's *capitalized* billings reflect the fact that it had double the gross income of ABC and can show a capitalized billing of $2 million compared with ABC's billing of $1 million.

This is standard procedure in the industry. So, if your gross income is more than 15 percent of billings, always give yourself a break and quote capitalized billings whenever you are asked about your agency's size. It will give you a number you can report that is larger than your actual billing.

When we consult with smaller agencies, most agency owners will apologize for their small billing number, which makes it hard to compete with other larger agencies (who may be capitalizing their billings). When we capitalize their billing, it gives them a better business profile and therefore greater confidence in going after new business. *Advertising Age*'s annual agency issues show all agencies with capitalized billing so that all agencies can be compared on an even playing field. In some cases, capitalization has doubled or even tripled their billing figure. It's amazing what it does to an agency's level of confidence. Principals and sales representatives are more positive when talking about the agency . . . especially in making new business presentations.

Gross Income

As pointed out above, gross income is the total amount of money the agency has to meet its own operating expenses including payroll and all other compensation. The customary definition is that gross income is the total of:

- commissions from media (and from other suppliers) retained by the agency, *plus*

- markups or other percentage charges added on to suppliers' bills by the agency, *plus*
- amounts billed for the time spent by agency personnel directly on behalf of the client, *plus*
- fees billed by the agency

Another way to arrive at the same figure is to take the total amount billed to the client for media, production (including any amounts for inside time), and fees and then subtract from that the amounts paid to media and *outside* suppliers for furnishing the materials and services for which you are billing your client.

Whichever of the two ways you prefer to determine your agency's gross income, the result will be exactly the same.

Gross income as defined above is the same for every agency, so you have a valid basis of comparison. Also, it's the best method of specifying the actual size of an agency as a going business. For these reasons, throughout this book all figures concerned with financial operations will be expressed as percentages of gross income.

Profit

When we start to define profit we run up against the idiosyncrasies of the federal tax laws plus the fact that the average agency is a highly personal business, usually owned and operated by very few individuals. This makes it possible for these principals to arrange payments to themselves in such a way as to minimize the tax bite—highly commendable, but a situation that tends to distort profit figures as normally defined.

An extreme example of this situation is the opportunity offered to corporations that qualify to elect to be taxed as partnerships. Under this method (Subchapter S), the owners pay taxes on their relative share of the corporation's profits. If the individual owner's tax rate is lower than the corporate rate, it obviously saves taxes, but plays havoc with making comparisons between agencies.

Operating Statement

A profit figure can be drawn off at any one of four places in a normal operating statement. The following example will illustrate these places and make it easier to understand the meaning and use of each of them.

Let's look now at the meaning and use of these different profit figures for a regular corporation.

XYZ Agency
Operating Statement

Total Billed to Clients	$5,000,000
Less: Paid to Media and Suppliers	4,000,000
Gross Income	$1,000,000
Expenses:	
Payroll—Principal Owners★	$ 80,000
Payroll—Staff	447,200
Non-Payroll Expenses	272,800
	$ 800,000
Gross Profit	$ 200,000
Less:	
Bonus—Principal Owners	$ 25,000
Bonus—Staff	95,000
Profit Sharing—Principal Owners	5,000
Profit Sharing—Staff	$ 25,000
Profit Before Taxes	$ 50,000
Less: Income Taxes★★	$ 7,500
Net Profit	$ 42,500

★ Principal Owners are usually defined as persons owning 10 percent or more of the agency.
★★ Income tax figures are for purposes of illustration only and are calculated at current rates.

Gross profit (gross income). This is very easy to define. It is simply the amount of money the agency has left from its operations, out of which to pay taxes and such optional benefits as year-end bonuses and profit sharing. How much this figure means, however, when comparing one agency with another depends on the business philosophy of the principal owners. Some prefer to operate by paying themselves only nominal salaries during the year with a whopping bonus near the end of the year. Therefore, this particular measure of agency profitability is of little value for smaller agencies where one or two owners may represent a quarter of the total employees. Its value as an effective comparison increases as agencies grow. After an agency reaches the approximate size of the XYZ Agency, which would be, typically, two principal owners and sixteen staff employees, the figure begins to take on real meaning as a measure of distributable profits.

Profit before taxes. This is the profit left after making all discretionary bonus and profit sharing payments and from which only federal income taxes need be deducted before arriving at the final profit available for payment of dividends and additions to surplus. Presumably at this point you've made all the discretionary payments necessary to keep your key people—and yourself—reasonably happy. Except in very unusual cases this figure represents the best measure of an agency's operations.

Note two things about this figure. First, only federal income taxes remain to be paid from it. When I say this I'm assuming that any state and city taxes have been deducted as part of regular operating expenses. This is proper because there are as many different bases as there are different taxing authorities, and some of them are so constructed that some tax is owed even if you lose money! Also, to act as a measure of your operations, profits must be stated before taxes. There are many things completely unconnected with operations that can affect the total tax due and hence the net profit—tax loss carryovers and nonoperating income, to name just two examples.

Net profit. This, too, is easily defined as the amount left over for the owners to use as they wish after all expenses and taxes have been paid. This is the figure commonly used for the listed stocks of major companies, but I don't think it's the best one for agencies. Principals who are practicing good tax planning may show little net profit while building up the value of the agency by reinvestment.

Proprietary profit. This is a new term designed to permit the evaluation of an agency whose owners regularly engage in tax minimizing. Proprietary profit is the sum of the salaries of principal owners *plus* the bonuses to principal owners *plus* net profit. The use of this concept will make allowances for the owners who adjust their own salaries up or down according to their personal needs for current income and the need of the agency to accumulate surplus.

Summary

Gross profit or *gross income* is the principal measure of agency size and all operating figures will be expressed as percentages of gross billing.

Profit before taxes is the normal figure used to represent the results of operations.

Net profit is what's left over after paying all expenses, all taxes, and all other miscellaneous expenses.

Proprietary profit will be used as a measure only when dealing with areas (such as agency valuation for merger or otherwise) where tax planning may be a factor.

How Much Profit?

Twenty percent of income is what an agency should make, but published figures average a lot less. Why? If 20 percent is unrealistic, what should an agency earn?

This is a good question, but not one that can be answered categorically. You'll recall that in the introductory chapter of this section I didn't use a single formula, but developed a table showing typical major expenses at different levels of profit. You pick the profit you want to achieve and then control your expenses so you do reach it at the end of the year.

"Well," you say, "that's fine, but how do I know what my target should be? How do I know if the target I pick is reasonable or if I'm dreaming?"

First consider what profit is meant to do. There are three principal goals. (My list is not in order of importance because priorities are always changing and depend on the agency's stage of growth.)

One goal certainly is to build up the strength of your agency. Accumulate the necessary working capital and the resources to withstand normal short-term business crises. Give the agency a basis for seeking credit, if necessary, and the wherewithal to take any available discounts.

A second major need for profit is to pay the owners of the agency for their contributions to its operations and also to reward them for the risks of ownership they're taking. Of course you undoubtedly pay yourself a salary, but if you're like most owners of small agencies I know, you'll set your current salary at a modest level and then take from profit enough to bring your yearly total up to what it should be. But to do this you must have a profit!

The other principal use for profit is to give a little extra reward to the staff who has worked for and with you all year. This can be a bonus or profit sharing but, again, the profit has to be there first!

Well, you may say, how about Uncle Sam? He's surely going to share in the profits. True enough, but no one in his right mind would earn a profit just so he could pay some taxes. Paying taxes is not one of the purposes of making a profit but, rather, an involuntary sharing of profit. This, of course, modifies all the numbers, but there are many things you can (and should) do to minimize taxes.

So, to set your profit goal for the year, start at the bottom and work up. Figure out how many dollars you must set aside to increase the strength of your agency. Some guidelines relating capital to agency size are discussed in Chapter 11. Let's say you settle on $50 thousand. This is 5 percent of gross income for the typical agency I've been using as an example.

This is net profit (that is, after taxes), so to get the corresponding profit before taxes, which, you'll remember, is the basic measure I'm using, you do a little mathematics based on the tax rate (15 percent in this example) and come up with a profit before taxes of $58,800. This is 5.88 percent of your $1 million gross income. So here's your starting point.

Profit Before Taxes	$58,800
Income Taxes	9,700
Net Profit	$49,100

How about reasonableness? Is the old 20 percent rule of thumb an attainable reality or a pipe dream? Let's look at the record compiled by agencies whose operating statements I have studied over a period of years. This chart shows an average profit of 3.86 percent of gross income.

The profits of these agencies were distributed as follows:

Profit Before Taxes as % of Gross Income	*% of Agencies*
More than 20%	4.48%
15%–20%	6.19
10%–15%	12.78
5%–10%	26.29
0%–5%	37.87
Lost Money	12.39
	100.00%

So 20 percent is an attainable goal. It may not be an easy goal to reach, but nothing really worthwhile is easy.

How Is Profit Divided?

In the last section I mentioned briefly the three major uses to which profits are put and said that the priorities between them vary with the stage of an agency's development. Let's look into each of these a little more closely.

Capital

When an agency is just starting out, the most important use for the agency's profit is to build up its capital to make it a sound business operation. You need working capital equal to about three months' payroll (or about 14 percent to 17 percent of gross income) plus enough to finance your few fixed assets such as furniture and equipment plus some more to represent a cushion against temporary slow periods. All of these would indicate a need for capital equal to about 25 percent to 30 percent of your gross income.

Once you reach this figure you probably won't want to add much more capital except as it's needed to finance further growth. Remember, an agency is a people business. It's much more important to invest in people than to build a big surplus once you've built up enough to let you take any discounts offered and have a modest cushion against a rainy day. But remember that until you reach this point, it's of utmost importance to strengthen the agency by retaining profits.

Staff Rewards

Since the whole success of an advertising agency depends on its people, you have to keep them happy and productive—and this usually comes right down to a question of money. There are two general philosophies in this area. One is to pay your people what you have to—in your market and in these times—and pay yourself, as owner, whatever is left over. The other way (which I prefer) is to pay your staff on a day-to-day basis just a little less than they could command in the open market and then share with them an extra reward at the end of the year. This is a matter of personal judgment, but it's been shown that a modest part of profits devoted to sweetening the pot for your people each year can pay big dividends in increased loyalty and productivity.

Ownership Rewards

The owners of most small- to medium-size agencies are hard-working sincere people who expect to take only enough income out of the agency each year to meet their current needs and still have some left over to build up the value of their investment in the business.

So, in fact, the owners' take from the business is a combination of current salary and profits retained in the business. Fortunately, the tax laws offer a fair degree of latitude as to how you do this to give yourself the maximum combined income and retained agency profits while minimizing corporate taxes.

The things to take into account are the corporate tax rate and your own effective tax rate after counting all proper deductions, exemptions, and so on. Remember, as Mr. Justice Holmes pointed out, the law requires no one to pay one penny more tax than is due. Tax evasion is not to be countenanced, but tax avoidance by following the letter of the law is financial planning of the highest order.

— 7 —

How Should You Charge for
Your Services?

Because an advertising agency is a *service business* that relies on the creativity and other services of staff, it is important to know how much it costs to deliver a job. Changes are taking place in how agencies charge for their services:

- The trend is toward retainer or service fees to cover agency service (replacing the 15 percent).

- More and more media are allowing the 15 percent agency commission to most any advertiser, which many times eliminates the need of the agency placing the advertising.

- New house agencies are on the increase . . . they are also requesting the agency commission, and getting it.

It is well established nowadays that advertising agencies have to gross more than the 15 percent on billings of the so-called commission system. What is not clear, however, is what services come under the remuneration provided by commissions and what extra ones have to be charged for in the form of fees or markups beyond this set percentage. Is there any well-established procedure accepted by agencies and clients alike, or is it still quite indefinite? Do agencies just charge what they can get? If so, isn't this a self-defeating practice?

As I pointed out in Chapter 2, there are only two ways in which you, as an agency principal, can have any influence on profit. One is to increase agency income, or at least see to it that income is reasonable in view of the services you offer, and the other is to control expenses. There just isn't any other way to affect profit. This chapter will cover the first of these factors—agency income—and the next chapter will talk about expenses.

The opening question indicates all the ways in which an agency can get paid for its services, and thus, serves as a splendid introduction to the problem of agency compensation.

To answer the broadest part of the question first—before branching out into a discussion of the different major ways in which an agency is paid for what it does—if total agency income is to be 20 percent of billing, the income from some activities must be far more than 20 percent to keep the total up to that level. The more an agency's billing is dependent on 15 percent commissions, the more aggressive it must be in getting top dollar for other services in order to get the total profit up to 20 percent of billing and more. Note that today's income figures are even getting higher than the standard 20 percent requirement.

COMMISSIONS

What services come under the remuneration provided by commissions? The answer to this question must be that commissions from media make up part of the income of most agencies and help to pay part of the cost of every service the agency provides. Way back in the beginning it might have been possible to say exactly what services media commissions paid for, but in today's complex multiservice agency it's really a meaningless exercise to try to say what source of income is supposed to pay for what service in whole or in part. What is important is the total agency income, not where it comes from.

For many years now media commissions have been standardized at 15 percent, with two major and some very minor exceptions. The two major ones are outdoor and transit advertising, where the commissions have previously run 16⅔ percent, and local rate advertising where no commission is allowed. In the latter case the almost universal practice is to gross it up by billing at the net local rate plus 17.65 percent to give the agency its 15 percent on the amount the client ends up paying.

Thus, with very few exceptions, the agency can expect an income of 15 percent on most of the media it buys and clients are accustomed to paying on this basis. It's almost unheard of for a client to object to any media bill assuming that the reproduction and other physical characteristics were acceptable, and that billing was at the scheduled rate. At the same time, you can't realistically expect an increase in the rate of media commissions because agencies are not doing anything for media that they haven't been doing for years. No increase seems warranted.

In the previous editions of this book, it was noted that the "commission system seems here to stay as a base." But how things have changed!

In January 1996, a report was made about the funeral of the 15 percent agency commission, which is another basic change that has affected agencies in the nineties. Here is an excerpt from the January 12, 1996, edition of *Advertising Age:*

> Now that the funeral for the 15 percent commission system is official, agencies must work hard to customize their compensation structures and find new ways of redefining their role in brand building.
>
> The Association of National Advertisers' "1995 ANA Trends in Agency Compensation" study revealed last week that only 14 percent of advertisers still use 15 percent commission-based payments, and agencies are increasingly moving toward labor fee and incentive-based setups.
>
> Indeed, some agencies that fought tooth and nail against the death of the once-standard 15 percent commission are finding that incentive-based programs are better for their profit margins. According to the ANA survey, some 45 percent of agencies are merely getting reduced-rate commissions.

Remember, these are large advertisers only that belong to ANA and do not represent all advertisers throughout the country. However, it is a trend to be reckoned with.

So we are back to how important it is to find other sources of income; for example: retainer fees, projects, cross merchandising, markups, surveys, focus study groups, and other sources.

Markups

In spite of being used for many years, there still seems to be some confusion about the 17.65 percent markup. What is a simple explanation? Also, to what kind of items do you usually add markups?

Both 15 percent taken off the gross media bill and 17.65 percent added on to a net bill produce exactly the same 15 percent income to the agency based on what the client pays. It's just the difference between discount and markup. Maybe a table will simplify the explanation.

	Commission Basis	Markup Basis
Billed to Client	$ 100	
Less: Commission	− 15	
Cost to Agency	$ 85	$ 85
Plus: Markup (17.65%)		+ 15
Billed to Client		$ 100

Thus, no matter how you figure it, the client pays $100 for something that costs the agency $85. When you start your calculation with cost you have to add $15 to reach the same bill to the client and this $15 represents 17.65 percent of the $85 cost to which it is added. It's just that simple! I know one agency that uses this language in its client agreement:

> We charge an amount which, when added to the net cost of media allowing no commission or less than 15 percent commission, will yield us 15 percent of our total media bill to you.

What's Marked Up?

Now let's turn to the question of what items are marked up and which are normally billed net. Generally, advertising materials and services purchased from outside suppliers are marked up. This category includes all the necessary mechanical elements that go into the final ad—artwork, film, and printing, for example, plus all the incidental steps taken along the way—computer graphics, color prints (or transparencies), scanning, and photo retouching, to name a few. The same is true of broadcast advertising except that here you may find a station selling both time and talent as a package, in which case the whole thing is usually subject to commission.

At the other end of the scale is a list of things that agencies never (well, hardly ever) mark up. These are all those out-of-pocket expenses incurred for specific clients that you simply try to recoup—such items as postage, long-distance telephone charges, faxes, photocopies, and travel. The one major item to which you never add a markup is a charge for time spent by any of your own people. It just makes no sense to bill $60 for an hour of an artist's time and then add a 20 percent markup when it's so easy to increase his rate to $72 and forget the markup. When you control the price, it's silly to irritate the client by adding on a markup when you can simply increase the price.

Then, finally, there's a big middle ground where no universal custom exists. Here you find such things as billing for research studies and store checks which you'll have to play by ear. If it's a relatively small job, you'll probably add a markup to the outside costs. If it's a big one you'll probably give your client a package price into which, of course, you'll build a markup for yourself.

How Much Markup?

"All this is fine," you say, "but what markup do I add to different items?"

There are two schools of thought on this. One school charges the same markup on all outside purchases and makes up the balance of needed income by adding fees of one sort or another. Agencies that follow this philosophy never mark up less than 17.65 percent and, in an increasing number of instances, use 20 percent, 25 percent, or even 33⅓ percent. At a recent meeting of one of the agency networks, a survey was taken to ascertain how much markup the members charged. The range went all the way from zip (because of fees) to 43 percent. The 17.65 percent markup seems to be losing ground.

The other school uses different markups for different kinds of jobs. Most of this group would use 17.65 percent on production to be used in media advertising, some would increase this to 20 percent for production used for low-cost trade paper advertising, and most of them would use 20 percent or higher on collateral jobs.

Even when agencies use this method they'll probably have some supplemental fees for different kinds of work. I prefer this policy of using different markups for different kinds of work. It ties the agency compensation much more closely to the work the client requires and thus is more equitable and easier to justify than a single flat markup.

So, while I can't provide a specific markup percentage, or even a series of them, I can point out one general principle that may help you set your own charges. This is that the farther you get from media advertising, the larger the markup needed. Almost everyone marks up non-commissionable media by 17.65 percent to come up with the normal

15 percent commission on all media. In trade magazine advertising the media is usually inexpensive and can't carry as large a percentage of the agency's cost, so the markup on production of trade ads tends to be somewhat higher. At the extreme end of this range of services is a collateral job with no media commission to help foot the bill, so the markup is almost always higher and is usually supplemented by a fee.

INTERNAL CHARGES

Does charging by the hour mean instead of, or in addition to, the 15 percent arrangement? How should this practice be carried out?

There is no questioning the fact that, with increasing costs for running an agency, the squeeze is on the commission system. We must either operate on a straight retainer basis, charging fees for our services, crediting our allowances from media against such fees to the client, or we must supplement our revenue from commissions by additional charges.

Charges in addition to commissions are of various types. The simplest, and perhaps the most widespread, is charging for computer-generated layouts done by your internal staff, even on commissionable accounts. Most of the smaller agencies and many of the largest do this.

Most agencies feel that an integral part of their service to clients, for which they are compensated by media commissions, is the development of the creative concept. By this they mean the writing of any copy and the production of a layout that is sufficiently finished so the client can see and approve the concept. Rough layouts are fast becoming another dinosaur in agency presentations. Now computer-generated graphics have taken over with highly talented creative people able to whip out comprehensive layouts in a fraction of the time and with dynamite colors. You must charge enough for this creativity and take into consideration time, equipment costs, depreciation, leasing, fees, etc.

Most agencies charge for writing copy—again especially in the case of industrial clients in which the copy may be long and technical.

There's a long list of assignments given to agencies for which there is no media commission whatsoever. At the head of the list are collateral jobs such as catalogs, brochures, and annual reports. If there's a big print run that the agency gets to handle, maybe the markup on that will be enough to cover costs and produce a profit, but chances are the client will handle the printing directly. So the agency must charge for the time all (and I mean *all)* of its people put in on the project.

Other activities the agency staff may be asked to undertake and that must be paid for under special arrangements would include complicated promotional jobs consisting not only of difficult and expensive-to-prepare technical trade advertising, but also elaborate point-of-purchase materials, publicity releases, and even general public relations counsel. For such jobs, the agency must receive a fee or find itself badly in the red at the year's end.

How to Pay for Internal Charges

I've said it before, but it's so basic it bears repeating—all any agency has to sell is the time and talent of its people. So, the agency's cost of one of these jobs handled internally has to be based on the time used by different people and their salary levels (as determined by their talents).

Hourly Rates

The simplest and most direct way to charge for internal time is by using hourly rates applied to the time each person spends on the job. Each employee's hourly rate is customarily based on a standard year of 1,600 hours (which allows for vacations, holidays, a few days home with the flu, and coffee breaks), and his basic hourly rate is his salary divided by 1,600. So, a $32,000-a-year employee has a basic rate of $20.00.

There's more to it than this, however, because every one on the staff generates overhead; hence, each dollar of direct salary is charged with its proportionate share of overhead. I'll talk about overhead at some length in the next chapter, but at the moment let's say that each $1.00 of direct expense has to carry $1.174 of overhead—which is a pretty good average. The real hourly cost of our $32,000 artist, then, is $20.00 plus $23.48, or $43.48. But, this is just your cost and you want to make a profit.

If you're shooting for the recommended 20 percent profit on gross, you'll have to mark your cost up by 25 percent (the same old 15 percent versus 17.65 percent gambit) and this adds another $10.87 to the hourly cost. All of which gives you a billing rate of $54.35.

At 2.718 times basic salary this is within the range of 2.5 to 3.0 that many agencies use as a multiplier to convert salaries into billable rates. By all means adopt some such standard multiplier if you wish, but be sure to check it first by following the procedures discussed in Chapter 10. Every agency is different in how it keeps its records and accounts for its time, so don't run the risk of shortchanging yourself by not checking first.

If you are looking for a much simpler way of billing for staff time, simply take the raw salary (as per sample above where you are paying a $32,000 employee $20 per hour), and multiply the basic payroll cost by three to five times. You could conceivably bill $60 to $100 per hour depending on the creative level and difficulty of handling this job.

Creative Fee

Many agencies normally charge a creative fee in addition to the other forms of charging for internal services. This is usually meant to cover the services of the top creative people who will be involved in general supervision of the creativity on a project even though they devote almost no direct time to it. It's usually expressed as a flat dollar charge per job.

Job Fee

Some kinds of jobs, particularly large research projects, can best be paid for by means of an overall fee worked out in advance with the client. Such a fee should cover the cost of services supplied by outsiders, reimbursement for the time your own people will put in on the job, and, of course, a profit for the agency. When working out such a fee, be very careful to spell out who is to do what and provide for some kind of adjustment or escape hatch in case conditions change.

In summary, I feel, by and large, that charging hourly rates for the hours actually devoted to a specific job is the best way to be reimbursed for time spent internally on billable activities. It's a system that can be used under any circumstances and it's one that ensures the agency of a profit on every hour that's billed. The other methods mentioned meet specific needs but, in the long run, are far less flexible.

RETAINER FEES

Accountants, doctors, lawyers, and other professionals all charge their clients fees for professional services. Why don't advertising agencies do the same thing? The answer goes way back to the early days of agencies when they were really space brokers and in no sense professionals. As their business became more complicated and they were called upon to supply more and more specialized services, agencies increasingly took on professional aspects.

So, when agencies were forced to increase their income to meet rising costs, most of them turned to fees either as a supplement to income from commissions and markups or as a replacement for them. Many multimillion dollar accounts are handled on an overall fee basis.

In the previous section I wrote about fees charged for certain types of jobs and others, such as creative fees, used for specific projects. What I'm talking about here is an overall retainer fee. This kind of fee can be in addition to all commissions, markups, and charges for inside time that the agency retains, or it can be much larger, completely replacing all other sources of agency income. It doesn't really make any difference so long as the total income compensates the agency for what it does and gives it a profit.

How Are Retainer Fees Calculated?

The classic retainer fee is stated as so much per month or year or whatever period you wish. Its amount is usually set by mutual agreement between the client and the agency. But this is just the end product; you'd better have some hard facts and figures to back you up in negotiating the fee. Your cost system, covering your overall operations and those on behalf of the client, must include these figures:

- An estimate of the salary cost for the time needed by the right number of the people with the skills necessary to do what the client needs to have done.
- An accurate estimate of the overhead associated with the salary cost.
- A provision for take-home pay for the principals that bears some resemblance to what they could earn in the open market. (This is calculated as part of the overhead factor.)
- Enough year-end profit to let you meet your goals.

How About Adjustment?

It would be a major miracle if the fee agreed upon by you and your client produces even a reasonable facsimile of the expected profit, no matter how good your intentions and how accurate your record keeping. Plan from the beginning to review the fee periodically and make any adjustments necessary. It will be easier to do this if you and the client have agreed on exactly what the fee covers: services to be performed, the people who will be involved, and the number of hours they will spend on the project.

If you set down exactly what you will provide in time and services, you can provide for adjustments with a clause in your agreement like this one:

> The fee should provide the Agency with a profit before taxes of 20 percent of the amount billed to the client:
>
> a. If the profit exceeds 20 percent, half of the excess will be refunded.
>
> b. If the profit is less than 20 percent, the agency shall receive a supplementary fee equal to half of the deficiency.

Another adjustment clause says simply:

> The agency's monthly cost accounting report, based on individuals' daily time sheets, will be the basis for the fee computation.

Other Ways of Figuring Fees

Besides the mutually agreed upon fee, there are two other common ways of setting up an overall retainer fee. The first might be called *hourly rate fee.* This is exactly the same as the method previously described for billing for services performed by artists, writers, and the like. The only difference is that when billing is on a total hourly rate basis, the time of everyone from the owner to the mail-room clerk is tallied and billed.

The other fee method is *cost plus,* under which all agency expenses including time and out-of-pocket are totaled, a profit factor is added, and the total is billed as a fee.

I don't really like either of these methods, basically because of the invitation to inefficiency and waste that's inherent in any cost plus system. But they do exist and, if properly controlled, can ensure a profit for the agency—if it doesn't go overboard and lose the whole account.

YOU MUST HAVE SUPPORTING DATA

The minute an agency starts charging for anything more than commissions and strictly mathematical markups, that is, as soon as it starts to bill for inside time and any sort of fee, it should be prepared to justify its charges with facts and figures.

The first requirement, without which no amount of facts will prevail, is to have a satisfied client. He or she must be convinced that your knowledge of his business, your professional skills, and your diligence in applying them on his behalf are giving him the kind of counsel best suited to his business needs. With this favorable client attitude the battle's half won; without it, you'll soon lose the account anyway.

I've already mentioned the second requirement—a sound cost system. In addition to providing the basis for estimating and setting fees, it's an absolute necessity for justifying your charges. At some point even the happiest client, probably prodded by auditors, stockholders, or competing agencies, is going to ask you to justify a fee. Some agencies I know beat the client to the punch and regularly go over with him their cost figures on his account. If you're sure of your figures (and don't do it if you're not!) this can build confidence and goodwill and may even get you an increased fee if your profit isn't all it should be.

The last, but probably most important, kind of support you need is a system of accurate time records showing who spent what time on which account. This brings us back to the fact that the time and talent of its people is the only thing any agency has to sell. If you don't know how your time is used, you're flying blind and can't charge clients what you're entitled to charge.

Of course, keeping accurate time sheets presents a problem. Agency personnel, usually enthusiastic and emotional, don't like numbers and hate to run in financial harness. Well, tell them that the one bunch of numbers they're sure to like—those on their pay-, bonus, and profit-sharing checks—depends entirely upon the agency's knowing how much money it is making, and that it operates in the dark without their cooperation in turning in accurate time records. Don't expect them to keep accurate time sheets just because you tell them to do so. They won't. They will, however, if their personal interests are involved.

Here's an example of how I once handled the problem of employees not filling out time sheets: When payday came around, no checks were given to those employees who did not complete their time sheets. When they came charging into my office to complain, I nonchalantly reminded them that because there were no time sheets from which to bill the clients, we were not able to bill the projects they worked on. That solved the problem of the missing time sheets.

PUBLISH YOUR TERMS

Most agencies, when making a presentation to a prospective client, suddenly become shrinking violets when the time comes to let the client know what services cost. Once it has been settled that the agency is desirable, from the client's viewpoint, and clearly capable of doing a good job, the question of financial arrangements should be tackled then and there; diffidence can only cause trouble later on. Actually, a client can feel only increased respect for an agency that insists on clarification of the financial arrangement before it concentrates on the professional relationship.

Not only should a well-run agency be happy to talk about its charges, it should have a price list (often called standard billing terms) printed up for distribution to all clients. This is a measure of professionalism that saves a lot of headaches. A client will pay almost any bill if he's expecting it; it's the unexpected bill that causes trouble.

An outstanding example of a price list (called "Working Arrangement" by the Chicago agency that uses it) is broken down into six broad functional areas:

- general advertising
- sales promotion
- publicity and public relations
- research and market analysis
- special assignments
- postage, telephone, fax, and copying charges

Each of these broad areas is subdivided into the different media or materials involved and the service to be performed with regard to each. The charge for each is then clearly shown as no charge, net cost, standard hourly rates plus cost of materials, or creative fee, as the case may be. This list covers six full pages and is supplemented by a dated sheet showing current hourly rates for different functions. There should be no unexpected bills from this agency!

At the end of this chapter is a suggested price list for various services.

WRAP-UP

The whole question of agency income turns out to be not a series of rigid percentages or methods of charging, but a set of basic financial management principles:

- Determine the income you need to cover expenses and provide a reasonable profit.
- Choose any combination of income sources—commissions, markups, internal charges, or fees—that will work best in your market and for your particular list of clients; and remember each client can be handled on a tailor-made basis if you want.
- Have a record-keeping system that will unmistakably prove the correctness of your charges.
- Tell your client ahead of time what your basis of charging is, review operations with him periodically, and show a willingness to make adjustments so the charges are fair to both you and the person who pays the bills.

Wise advertisers select agencies that offer outstanding abilities in advertising and marketing. They expect the agency's output to reflect these abilities in originality, initiative, and sound reasoning.

As in all things, in the long run you get what you pay for. Just as advertisers need to realize that cheap advertising services are invariably the most expensive in the long run, so agencies must recognize their own value and refuse to sell themselves for less money than can show a decent profit.

Clients that do not provide an agency with a reasonable profit must have their charges increased or be dropped. The only alternative, if the agency is not to lose money on these clients, is to cut down on services. This hurts both the advertiser and the agency in very short order. Only the best advertising succeeds in these increasingly competitive days.

In conclusion, set your profit first, charge enough to produce it, and above all, be ready to prove unmistakably that your charges are justified. Any client who is not willing to pay fair sums for services rendered should get another agency.

Here is a typical list of hourly rates for agency services. You may want to adjust these rates to your specific situation and geographic area.

Concept and creation of original ideas: $250 and up
(there is a service fee charged in addition to the following charges)
Layout: $75 to $90
Production coordination: $55 to $70
Copywriting: $75 to $100
Keyline (mechanicals): $55 to $75
Finished art: $75 to $250
(depends upon degree of involvement)
Art direction for photo shoots: $60 to $75
Account executive time: Charge from three to five times basic salary.
(Divide 1,600 hours into annual salary to determine hourly rate you are paying.)

— 8 —

How to Allocate
Your Gross Income

MANAGING GROSS INCOME

In order to be able to control agency finances, it is essential to have an understanding of the terminology of agency finance. Here are some ABCs:

Most agencies are classified, measured, and ranked in terms of billings. I suggest that you forget about billings and think in terms of *gross income* (also known as *gross profit*). The reason is that after paying all direct costs (media, printing, photography, all out-of-pocket expenses related to servicing the accounts), gross income is the only money you have left to manage your business. This goes for payroll, rent, utilities—everything it takes to operate your business. (A detailed breakdown of monies to be taken out of gross income follows.) After you have paid all these expenses, the money you have left over is *net profit*. So, how you manage the gross income dollars will determine the financial success of your business.

Another reason why this is so important is that the real value of an agency or design studio is determined by the gross income. When agencies are purchased and sold, the price is almost always based on the gross income, not the gross billing.

Here are the costs that must come out of your gross income:

Salaries—account service, copy, art, media, traffic, production, accounting/EDP, general office administration, receptionist, secretarial, etc.

Other indirect overhead costs—auto expense, depreciation, dues and subscriptions, entertainment, gifts and donations, insurance–employee benefits, insurance-operating, interest and bank charges, legal and accounting, office expense, other taxes and licenses, payroll taxes, promotion, rent, repairs and maintenance, supplies for art and office, telephone, temporary help, travel, entertainment, unbillables, and miscellaneous.

The bottom line: *Think gross income.* Keep all the above costs within your gross income and you will *earn a net profit* for your company.

An agency's basic philosophy should be to set aside profit first and spend on operating expenses only what's left. How should you classify these expenses, and what are reasonable standards for each of them?

First, this basic philosophy represents the only way an agency can be sure of making a profit. This holds true even if a year comes along—as it will for most agencies—when good business judgment tells you that some things may be more important that year than a profit—like keeping on a few key people even in the face of reduced billings so you can keep up your standards of service. The point is that you're on solid ground only if you make that decision with your eyes open. That way you're still in control.

The previous chapter discussed the different sources of agency income; this one concerns operating expenses, the only other factor that has an effect on profits. This is probably the most important factor in planning for profit because you have much greater control over expenses than over income.

TOTAL EXPENSES

Once you've determined the profit you want to make, you have also decided what your total expense will be because the formula is:

$$\text{Income} - \text{Profit} = \text{Expenses}$$

There are two ways in which this total expense is broken down for purposes of control. They are, first, payroll and nonpayroll expenses; and, second, direct and indirect expenses. These two classification systems overlap, but they serve different purposes and each is vital to sound agency management. Basically, the payroll/non-payroll breakdown is used for budgeting and controlling the agency's operations as a business. The direct/indirect breakdown is used for cost accounting to determine and control operations on behalf of specific clients. Each of these is discussed in the remaining sections of this chapter.

PAYROLL EXPENSE

Agencies, after all, are only people, and, as you'd expect, payroll is far and away the major item of expense. Agency expense for payroll should average 50 to 60 percent of gross income.

So when you're setting up your budget, first decide how much profit you want, then figure out from the table in Chapter 5 approximately how much you can spend for payroll based on your projected income. Set that percentage as your goal and watch it like a hawk each month. All agency expenses are related to people, and if you keep the people expense in line, chances are everything else will be in line too, including your profit.

How to Control Your Overhead

If you follow the right numbers, you will be guaranteed a profit. It's that simple . . . and that difficult! After you have paid your direct costs (media, outside production, freelance, and expense related to the direct expenses of handling the job for a client) you have your gross income. It's important to remember that these are the only dollars you have to run your shop. Consider your gross income as 100 percent—your *total* dollars. Then allocate the following percentages to these expense categories: payroll—50 percent (includes the principal's salary); overhead—30 percent (includes rent, utilities, all expenses related to operating your office); and profit—20 percent.

There are so many variations in agency operations; sometimes more emphasis is placed on account service, while another shop may be creative and production oriented. The following figures are merely a composite of all agencies and will give you a guide to set your own percentages.

Typical Breakdown of Agency Payroll and Related Expenses

(as percentages of total payroll)

Direct:

Contact	29.29%	
Creative	24.69	
Implemental and Production	17.23	
Total Direct		71.21%

Indirect:

General and Administrative	12.65	
Executive Overhead	16.14	
Total Indirect		28.79

Total Payroll and Related Expenses   *100.00%*

Here are definitions of each of these functional payroll categories:

Account Service (Client Contact)—the formulation of plans and usually merchandising and public relations, meeting with client

Creative—conception of ideas, copywriting, design of graphics and illustrations.

Implemental and Production—all those activities necessary to get advertising message into the media, such as film, videotapes, finished art.

General Office—all those activities necessary to keep the office running, practiced by such people as messengers, receptionists, switchboard operators, accountants, secretaries, and the like.

Executive Overhead—includes the time the principal spends in directing the operations of the agency and also the time spent on new business by all staff members. If you want to show this separately, it must be combined with other administrative payroll for purposes of analysis.

Secretarial—the one large group not included so far is the secretarial staff, which is handled in one of two ways. Smaller agencies tend to list them as general administrative people, while larger ones usually put them in the same category as general office.

There are two ways you can list payroll figures to compare them with these guidelines. The person who does nothing but write copy goes under Creative no matter which method you use. But the multitalented individual who contacts the client, writes some copy, and handles the media recommendations presents a problem. You can list him under what you think his primary function is and ignore the others for budget purposes or you can make an approximation of how he divides his time and divide his salary the same way—maybe 45 percent to Contact, 30 percent to Creative, and 25 percent to Implemental.

If you use the method of putting a person's entire salary in a single category, you should adjust the basic guideline figures accordingly to reflect your method of operation.

Of course, if you allocate a higher percentage for one function you must allocate less for others so you won't go over the total payroll percentage for the profit you're planning to make.

Whichever way you choose, be consistent and use the same system across the board.

In all of this, however, remember that every agency is different, so this sample distribution of payroll between different functions can be considered only as a guide. As long as you stay within your goal range for total payroll, you can shift payroll from one function to another at will, as best serves the needs of your clients. You can even make shifts between payroll and nonpayroll expenses as long as you stay within the total expense figure you've set for yourself.

NONPAYROLL EXPENSE

The broad category of nonpayroll expense generally represents just under 29 percent of an agency's total expenses and somewhere between 23 percent and 27.3 percent of its gross income. It is sometimes loosely referred to as overhead, but I think that's incorrect. There's a special section on overhead at the end of this chapter.

Just as people are expected to perform certain functions in the planning, creating, and placing of advertising, nonpayroll expenses are incurred in the performance of certain functions vital to the operation of the agency as a business. Following are four major functions of this sort (plus the catchall "miscellaneous"). By combining into these functional groupings the 20-odd expense categories that seem to be the accepted industry standard, we do away with the exercise in futility of riding herd on an expense item that may run one-tenth of one percent of income. For a typical agency with a gross income of $1 million, that's only $1,000—so, even if that item increases by 50 percent it's gone up only $500.

Here are the major functional categories of nonpayroll expense I like to use and a list of what goes into each. The categories are the same as are now used by the American Association of Advertising Agencies.

Client Service Expense

This category includes all expenses incurred for the benefit of specific clients. The major components are travel and entertainment and the cost of research and other items that may not be able to be billed to the client. The cost of these services should normally run from 3 percent to 6 percent of gross income. Faxing and photocopying expenses could fall into this category.

Space and Facilities Expense

This expense provides for the physical surroundings in which you work. Rent is almost always the largest single item. You also include any maintenance or repair costs you incur, heat and light, a depreciation fund to replace worn-out equipment, and insurance to shield you from losses. If you rent office machines, furniture, or the like, you put those expenses here, too. If you own your own building—as many agencies do, particularly in smaller cities—you include mortgage interest, real estate taxes, and other costs of operating the building. Also included are the cost of such facilities and services as postage, telephone, data processing, and such items as stationery and office supplies, and the purchase of minor pieces of equipment. This category should normally run 13 percent to 17 percent of gross income.

Corporate Expense

This category represents the cost of general corporate activities such as the agency's own advertising, donations, provision for doubtful accounts, interest paid, memberships, dues and subscriptions, and new business expenses. In total this category normally costs between 4 percent and 7 percent of gross income.

Professional Fees

This category covers fees paid to your accountant, your attorney, and any other management service fees you may incur. It should run from 1 percent to 2 percent of income.

Summary

As with all the figures in this chapter, the ranges above are only guidelines that must be adjusted for each agency's operation. For example, if you move to suburbia, or even exurbia, to escape the high-rent district, you can reduce your facilities expense, but as a result, you'll probably have to spend more on travel to see your clients, so that expense can be expected to go up. However, travel and contact time costs have been reduced significantly with the increased use of faxes, E-mail, voicemail, and computer-generated layouts and copy. The important thing is to adjust as needed between categories to reflect your own operating style while keeping the total in line with your planned profit.

Thus, in a nutshell, the breakdown of total expenses into payroll and nonpayroll categories lets you determine the total cost of each function performed by your people and also the cost of each physical function needed to provide tools and a place to work. At this point you're concerned with the function and its cost, not whether it is being performed for one or more specific clients or for the agency itself.

DIRECT AND INDIRECT EXPENSE

In addition to knowing what each agency function costs, it's important to know how much of the cost of each function is devoted directly to activities for specific clients and how much goes to keeping the agency running as a business enterprise. Without information of this sort you have no way of comparing the cost of handling a client's business with the income you get from that client. Consequently, you can't tell which accounts are profitable (and by how much) and which are costing you money and require special attention.

This brings us to the second major way of classifying agency expenses—direct and indirect. Each of these categories will include some payroll expense and some nonpayroll expense. The distinction is that every item of expense incurred to serve a specific client is direct expense, while expenses connected solely with agency operations are classified as indirect.

For example, the president of an agency might spend 25 percent of his or her time contacting specific major accounts and another 10 percent in writing copy for those same clients. These, of course, are direct expenses. At the same time the president may spend 30 percent of his or her time on new business activities and the remaining 35 percent in general administrative duties. Each of the two latter activities is considered part of executive overhead, so each $1,000 of the president's salary would be distributed as follows:

Client Contact	$250	
Creative	100	
Direct Payroll Expense		$ 350
Executive Overhead (Indirect Payroll)		650
		$1,000

Almost every staff member will have both direct and indirect time and it's desirable to record the distinction whenever possible. About the only exceptions are accounting people, receptionists, and the like, almost all of whose time is indirect.

On the other hand, an account executive who you'd think would have only direct time will have indirect time when he's pursuing new business or running some personal errands. You should try to segregate as much direct time as you can without carrying it to ridiculous extremes. It's particularly important if you have clients on a fee basis under which you bill at hourly rates for the time of all people involved with the account.

If you analyze the work of all staff employees the same way I did that of the principal owners, you might find this breakdown of each $1,000 of staff payroll:

Contact Staff:	
Client Contact	$ 750
New Business (Executive Overhead)	250
	$1,000
Creative Staff:	
Creative	$ 800
Administrative	100
New Business	100
	$1,000
Implemental Staff:	
Implemental	$ 850
Administrative	150
	$1,000
General Staff:	
Administrative	$ 700
Executive Overhead	300
	$1,000

Putting together the tables on pages 78 and 79, you would arrive at the breakdown of total payroll shown on page 81.

Most nonpayroll expenses are indirect, but some of large proportions can properly be classified as direct and charged against your operations for specific clients. The most obvious examples are long–distance telephone calls, faxes, photocopies, travel and entertainment, and unbillables such as errors. It's important to isolate these costs of serving specific clients not only to figure total cost per client but also to bill for some expenses when they've been isolated and documented.

By definition, client service expenses are always classified as direct expenses. Occasionally, however, some items of what is normally an indirect expense may be incurred for a special client project and should be moved into the direct category. If, for example, $500 of the telephone expense (normally included in space and facilities) was incurred for a specific client project, the total of nonpayroll expenses might look like this:

	Direct Client Expense	Agency Expense	Total
Client Service Expense	$45,700	—	$ 45,700
Space and Facilities Expense	500	$150,900	151,400
Corporate Expense	—	58,300	58,300
Professional Fees	—	17,400	17,400
	$46,200	$226,600	$272,800

All of these statements of expenses can be combined into a single one that would look like this:

Direct Payroll Expenses:			
Client Contact	$155,675		
Creative	135,960		
Implemental (Production)	99,110		
		$390,745	
Direct Client Expenses:			
Client Service Expense	$ 45,700		
Facilities Expense	500		
		46,200	
Total Direct Expenses			$436,945

continued

Indirect Payroll Expenses:			
General and Administrative	$119,560		
Executive Overhead	166,895		
		$286,455	
Nonpayroll Expenses:			
Space and Facilities	150,900		
Corporate	58,300		
Professional Fees	17,400		
		226,600	
Total Indirect Expense			513,055
Total Expense			$950,000

OVERHEAD

This usually misunderstood and much maligned term is often interpreted as the place to put any expense that's difficult to classify. A little analysis of why we want to determine an overhead figure will simplify the problem.

The dictionary defines overhead as "those general expenses in a business which cannot be charged up as belonging exclusively to any particular part of the work." This implies, of course, that there are expenses that can be charged up exclusively to some particular part of the work and, furthermore, that such charges would be different for different parts of the work. So, before we can define overhead we must decide the part of the work to which it is related.

The total work of the agency is to serve its clients by counseling them and producing and placing their advertising. So, the different parts of the work would seem to be the services rendered to each separate client. On this basis overhead is the total of those agency expenses that cannot be charged to specific clients. In other words it is the same as the indirect expenses discussed in the preceding section. This includes, of course, both payroll and nonpayroll items. So, if we credit the agency with gross income of $1 million, its complete operating statement would look like this:

Agency Income		$1,000,000
Direct Expense	$436,945	
Indirect Expense	513,055	
Total Expenses		950,000
Profit Before Taxes		$ 50,000

Breakdown of Total Payroll

Function	Owners	Staff				Total
		Contact	Creative	Implemental	General	
Contact	$ 27,500	$128,175	—	—	—	$155,675
Creative	11,000	—	$124,960	—	—	135,960
Production	—	—	—	$ 99,110	—	99,110
Total Direct	$ 38,500	$128,175	$124,960	$ 99,110	—	$390,745
Administrative	—	—	$ 15,620	$ 17,490	$ 86,450	$119,560
Executive Overhead	$ 71,500	$ 42,725	15,620	—	37,050	166,895
Total Indirect	$ 71,500	$ 42,725	$ 31,240	$ 17,490	$123,500	$286,455
Total Payroll	$110,000	$170,900	$156,200	$116,600	$123,500	$677,200

Whenever the word "overhead" is used in this book, I will be talking about total indirect expenses—those expenses not incurred for any specific client but on behalf of all clients as a group. How this figure is used in reports and how it is distributed will be discussed in the section on Cost Accounting in Chapter 10.

— 9 —

Billing for Your Services

Billing is another function that gets lost or delayed in many small agencies. How many times have I heard, "We just have to get our billing out." Agency principals get so tied up with meeting clients and fighting deadlines that taking the time to do the billing becomes subordinate to getting the work done. See Chapter 2 for detailed instructions on timing your billing (and payments) so you are not paying your clients' costs.

SPECIAL KINDS OF MEDIA BILLING

Billing on closing dates does incur some problems, but it's one way to protect yourself. Newspaper ads may run with fewer lines than the insertion order calls for, and broadcast spots can be omitted or preempted or suffer power failures—so you don't really know what you have run until you get the proof of performance. In this kind of situation, is there any way to get your money? Yes, there is.

For these media adopt a one-line or commitment system of billing. Let's use TV spots as an example. At the end of the month you know what television spots you have ordered, and the client knows, too, from his copies of the schedules. What neither of you knows at this moment is just how many spots ran, but there's no doubt that you and the client are obligated to pay for the spots that did run.

You look at your schedule and find that you've ordered, say, $3,250 worth of spots for November. So, on November 30 you send the client a bill (due December 10) that simply reads: "TV Advertising Committed for November 19__: $3,250." No stations, no dates, no times—just a single amount.

This bill carries your usual terms and, if the client is well trained, he pays it. During the following month you get all the station bills, check and audit them, and prepare a detailed bill for the client. You send the client this toward the end of the month and show a credit for the one-line bill already paid. Then you start all over with a new one-line bill at the end of this month.

What if there are always some omissions and the client objects to being billed for the full amount scheduled when he knows he will get some money back? Easy. Just make the one-line bill equal to 90 percent of the commitment or whatever other percentage experience shows is about right for this client.

If the client doesn't want to pay in advance, point out that it's not paying in advance. The spots have been committed to run for that month. The only thing is that no one knows exactly what did run and so you are billing an estimated amount for the spots that already have run, that were authorized, and for which the client is obligated to pay.

Production Billing

Because production jobs can extend over several weeks—even months—and because many different suppliers are involved, it's almost impossible to bill your client in time to get paid before you have to pay your suppliers. You just don't know which supplier is going to bill you when and in what amount. While you can't completely eliminate paying suppliers before you get paid, there are some things you can do to reduce the burden of carrying the cost of work in progress.

Progressive Billing

At the end of each month agencies using this system list each payment made to suppliers on each active job in the house. The client is then sent a bill for each active job covering payments made to suppliers for that job during the month just ended. This means that the agency must write a lot of bills and the client must accumulate several bills for many jobs, but it does substantially reduce the work-in-progress costs the agency must carry.

Inventory Billing

Some clients object to having to process all the bills issued under progressive billing and ending up with several bills for a single job. They prefer the single bill sent only as each job is completed. These client benefits can be retained and the agency still relieved of financing the work-in-progress by using an inventory billing system.

Agencies that use this system list payments they make against each job number just as do those who use progressive billing. However, instead of sending out bills for these amounts, these agencies charge the amounts to an "inventory of work-in-progress" account with a separate listing for each job for each client. They then add up all the items listed for any one client at the end of the month and send out a bill that reads simply: "Inventory Accumulated for Your Benefit at the End of Month of _____: $7,460."

Any jobs that are completed during the next month are billed as usual and at the end of the month, you send the client a credit for $7,460, and the new bill for current inventory. So, you're really running a banking operation under which your client keeps on deposit with you enough money to finance its inventory.

Partial Billing

There's one other special kind of billing some agencies use on big collateral jobs that can go uncompleted for weeks or months. Under this system you bill one-third of the estimated cost when the job is authorized, another third when the proofs are approved, and the final third when the job is finished.

PROMPT PAYMENT PROBLEMS

So, you've done everything you can to establish practices that ensure your getting your money on time and still some clients drag their feet. Is there anything else you can do?

Friendly Persuasion

Most agencies I know rely heavily on the old theory that "the squeaky wheel gets the grease" and start calling the client as soon as a bill is due and not paid. Usually the account executive is given the responsibility for following through with clients. Make sure, though, that he or she realizes that the job is completed only when the money is in the bank and that, while the client must be pleased, the agency is of greater importance. The agency issues a paycheck and that's where his or her first loyalty should be.

Other agencies have their financial people get in on the act at some point. Still others count on their principals. Whoever does this, have them keep at it. An agency's profit margin is too low to let things slide.

Cash Discounts

Some media allow a 2 percent cash discount for payment by the agency within 10 days. When agreeing to pass this on to clients, be firm in your policy that 10 days means 10 days. To avoid any misunderstanding, it's probably well to convert this into a specific discount date. Instead of saying "Cash discount of 2 percent if paid in 10 days" say right on your bills "Cash discount of 2 percent if paid by January 10th" or whatever date is applicable. When a client firm passes up a discount, contact its treasurer and point out how much money it's losing by not taking the discount. Two percent for 10 days figures out to about 72 percent per year.

Credit Insurance

Credit insurance is intended to protect you against nonpayment of bills, but it can also help in cases of slow payment. A reminder to the client that your policy requires regular reports to a credit agency on past-due items can help speed things up.

Finance Charge

If a client wants you to act as a banker, he or she certainly should pay you for it. Like most department stores and major oil companies, many agencies are starting to charge 1½ percent or more per month on accounts that are overdue. I urge you not to finance the client, but it hurts a little less if you get paid for it!

STATE YOUR TERMS—NO SURPRISES!

I've said it before, but it's worth repeating. The bill that gives you most trouble is the unexpected bill. So don't keep your clients in the dark! When you're in the process of making your final pitch to a prospective client, come right out in the open and say, "We charge for this and this; the basis on which our charges are calculated is thus and so; our terms of payment are these." No advertiser is going to object to this kind of approach; in fact, he or she will probably respect you all the more for taking a sound businesslike approach to questions about money. Go one step further and prepare a rate card that spells out all your charges and distribute it freely to clients and prospective clients.

It is sad that many talented and creative agency principals have lost their agencies due to undisciplined billing. They are so wrapped up with serving clients and fighting deadlines that billing becomes secondary. *Don't let this happen to you!*

—10—

Insist on Getting Financial Reports Regularly

It's amazing how many small agency owners fail to get financial reports on time; many times, in fact, reports arrive too late to avoid a catastrophe!

Often an advertising agency will find it practically impossible to get any idea of how it is doing financially because the bookkeeper is so busy sending out bills and watching collections that financial reports don't get written. The agency is audited once a year by an outside accountant, and only then does it get any really accurate idea of where it is heading. Is this a normal state of affairs in our business and, if so, should it remain this way?

The answer to the first question is "Maybe" and to the second, "Absolutely not!" An agency cannot know where it is going if its financial status is unclear. To chart a financial course properly you, as agency principal, must know at all times and as accurately as possible just where the agency stands at any given moment and also how it got there over the past few months. This chapter will discuss the kinds of reports you must get and when you must have them if you intend to chart a sound financial course.

REGULAR MONTHLY REPORTS

Monthly reports are vital. It is astonishing how much can happen to an agency in only a month's time. The operation for this short period may amount to as much as the agency has in the world. An agency can be solvent one day and its principals can wake up the following morning and find it bankrupt. Every advertising agency should receive, no later than the tenth of every month, a financial report on its situation. This should be considered part of the bookkeeper's job, whether this person is an in-house employee or part of an outside financial service. I know of one agency principal who receives a financial update daily! He's really on top of his agency's financial status.

It is not enough to tell your bookkeeper, "We want to know where we stand every month." Provide a simple printed form worked out with the aid of the accountant who is responsible for the company's yearly audit. The spaces on this form indicate the information that must be forthcoming every month, and using the same form every month makes tracking your financial health easier because you can easily compare one month with the next. If you are using in-house computer-based accounting, you should be able to get reports and even graphs on a moment's notice. At a minimum, however, here are the reports you should get every month without fail.

Operating Statement

Another common name for the operating statement is profit and loss statement. It should show the figures for the current month and also for the period from the start of your fiscal year to the present. If you operate on the basis of agency budgets (which I recommend), a third column should show the budget for the year to give you a benchmark against which to measure your progress.

This statement is designed to answer three simple but vital questions:

- How much income did we receive?
- How much did we spend?
- How much did we make?

First, how much income did we receive last month? Don't confuse this with billings. This figure is the total of commissions, markups, and fees received. It should be at least 20 percent of dollar billings, and even this may turn out to be too low. This figure is not profit. It is gross income. It does not include cash discounts because these we extend to the client as earned, in dollar amounts, not percentages. If you wish, you may show the total amount you've billed your clients so you can check the percentage that gross income represents of the billing.

Likewise, you may want to show separately the income received from commissions, from markups, and from fees. But however you break it down for your own information, the important thing is to show total gross income, which is the benchmark against which everything is compared.

Second, how much did we spend on our various services and our agency operations out of this income? These expenditures should be broken down to show separately each of the five payroll categories and four nonpayroll categories of expense discussed in Chapter 8. By preparing your report in this form you can determine the percentage of gross income each major expense represents and then use these figures to check performance against the targets.

Third, how much did we make? Compare this each month with the profit goal you have set for the agency.

Balance Sheet

This is the statement that shows your financial status at the end of each month. Basically, it shows what you own and what you owe. Look critically at each of these figures, all the while asking yourself such questions as, "Are we really going to collect all those receivables, or are we daydreaming? Have we really allowed enough depreciation so our figure for furniture and fixtures represents a true present value?" Be realistic in your answers, for if you're kidding anybody, it can only be yourself.

Accounts Receivable

This extremely valuable statement should be drawn up separately for each client, and it should be aged. That is, list the oldest first. Go down this list with a firm resolve that you'll start screaming immediately about any items that are overdue. Don't let them build up!

Cost Accounting

The financial reports I've been talking about show how the agency as
a whole is doing and how well cost relates to income for major functions. This is fine as far as it goes, but you also need some way of knowing which clients are showing a profit, and how much, and which are
causing you to suffer a loss. In short, you need cost accounting.

A good cost system shows not only which accounts are causing a
loss (the accounts on which you should take corrective action) but
also how much correction is needed. In addition, there is bound to
come a time when you'll have to justify the fairness of the fees you
charge clients. And there's no way you can do that if you can't
demonstrate what your costs are. There are even some fee plans that
call for adjustments based on cost accounting.

Basic Form

A separate cost accounting statement should be made for each client
and should contain this kind of information:

Client A	Period	Year to Date
Gross Income	$ 50,000	$ 190,000
Direct Salaries	19,500	68,500
Share of Overhead	22,890	80,420
Direct Client Expenses	250	500
Total Expenses	$ 42,640	$ 149,420
Profit Before Taxes	$ 7,360	$ 40,580

When you've made a statement like this for every client, the total
of the profit or loss shown for each must add up to the bottom-line
figure on your operating statement for the same period.

Period Covered

Many agencies prepare cost accounting statements every month, but
I don't think that's necessary except in unusual circumstances. Normally, a quarterly report is sufficient, in which case your two columns
would be for the current quarter and for the period since the start of
your fiscal year.

Direct Salaries

The sample shows only a single salary figure, which you'll want to break down to show the salary cost of each function you perform—such as contact, creative, and the like. The more detail you show, the better control you'll have over your operations. Also, if you ever need to discuss fees with a client—and you probably will—you'll be on much sounder ground if you can specify what you did for him and what each function cost you.

Functional Time Sheets

The only way to tell how much direct salary to charge against each client is to have everyone who works an appreciable amount of time on an account turn in time sheets recording that time so it can be priced out. What you need to know is who spent how much time performing what function for which client. To have meaningful figures all these elements must be present.

Since you're concerned with functions, the time sheets must allow for recording not only the client served, but also the function performed. This means that a person who wears two hats must either use two separate time sheets, one for each function, or use a time sheet with different columns for different functions.

A final point about time sheets: they must be timely. It's awfully hard on Friday to remember accurately what you did on Monday, so the best system is to require time sheets to be turned in each day. If that can't be done, at least require that the time be recorded every day even if a longer period is covered by a single time sheet. Time spent on jobs can also be recorded by computer.

Direct Client Expenses

These are all those out-of-pocket items you have to incur in properly serving clients—travel, long-distance telephone calls, and charge-offs, to name just a few. Many of these items can readily be identified as being concerned with one specific client. They should appear on his or her cost accounting statement so it will reflect your true cost of serving that client. It's obviously unfair to charge all clients for an expense incurred for just one of them, which is what you do when you leave such expenses in overhead instead of charging them against the specific clients who benefited from them.

Overhead

I've already defined overhead as the total of an agency's indirect expenses. It's very simple to arrive at the total overhead when you're preparing your cost accounting statements. You add up for all clients the direct salaries you've figured for each of them plus the direct client expenses and subtract this total from the agency's total expense. What's left is overhead.

Now comes the question of how you allocate this overhead to your different clients. The three most widely used bases are gross income, direct time in hours, and direct salary costs.

The rationale behind allocation on the basis of gross income received from each client is that the agency's purpose in incurring overhead expenses is to receive income; hence overhead should be charged as that income is received. The big, and I think fatal flaw in this is that overhead expenses of an agency may bear no relationship whatever to income. A simple example will show what I mean. An agency may find that it can't handle a client's business at a reasonable profit so it seeks and gets a supplemental fee. The workload hasn't changed at all, no additional overhead costs are incurred, but the income the agency receives from this client has increased. So the client is penalized by being charged with more overhead and all other clients are benefited by overhead charge reductions. It can't really be justified.

The second widely used method is to allocate overhead on the basis of the hours of direct time devoted to each client. This is an improvement over the income basis because hours spent are related to work that must be done. This is all right for small agencies where almost everyone on the staff works on almost every account; unfortunately, it ignores the fact that some hours are worth more than others, whether in cost to the agency or value of services performed for the client.

The third method based on direct salary costs recognizes the different cost of hours put in by different people. Certainly an hour of the principal's time is worth more than an hour of an intern's. It's also true that the owner generates more overhead. He has a big office, he may have two telephones, and he needs and uses more clerical help. So there is a reasonable relationship between direct salary costs and the overhead needed to support them. What's more, the figures are readily available, which makes it simple to allocate the overhead. I advocate this method in all but very exceptional cases.

So, in practice, you would determine the total overhead and its allocation by this process:

Total Agency Expenses		$100,000
Direct Salary Expenses:		
Client A	$19,220	
Client B	15,190	
Client C	11,400	
	$45,810	
Direct Client Expenses	2,000	
Total Direct Expenses		$47,810
Overhead		*$56,130*

The $56,130 in overhead would then have to be allocated to the $45,810 of direct salary expenses and we would find Client A charged with $23,550, Client B with $18,612, and Client C with $13,968.

ESTIMATING

Regular operating and cost accounting reports tell you quite accurately where you are, but they are of much greater value if they can be compared with a budget showing where you expect to be and, thus, how near you are to reaching your goal. This calls for a good estimating system.

Start by having each account executive estimate what income you'll get from each of the clients he or she handles; estimate income by quarters. At the end of each quarter you'll know what income you actually received. Go over this record with the account executive, see where he or she has been unduly optimistic or pessimistic, and have him or her revise estimates for the balance of the year. Your account executive's accuracy should improve as the year progresses.

Knowing not only what income to expect, but when to expect it will be a big help in evaluating the regular reports. If you're expecting only one-third of your income in the first half year, you won't be unduly depressed if your profit looks a little sickly after the first six months. It works the other way, too. If your estimates show two-thirds of your income in the first half year, a realization of this will cool your exuberance over a hefty profit and keep your enthusiasm from letting you approve all sorts of expenditures.

The ultimate test of a sound estimating system comes in setting a fee for handling a client's total account. If you and the client agree on what's to be done—so many ads of this or that kind, for example—and if you know from your experience and your cost system what it will cost you to produce this work, you can set an overall fee that will be fair to both you and your client.

Furthermore, with a realistic income and expense goal as a target you can tell at any time where you are. If things are getting a little out of kilter, your cost system should let you demonstrate this to the client, so you both can agree on a correction before things get completely out of hand.

Even if you aren't on a complete fee system with a client, but charge a fee only for some unusual jobs, a good cost system, and the accurate estimating of costs that it allows, is worth its weight in gold.

There are no areas in agency work in which a sound cost system is so essential as it is on jobs for which the agency plans to charge a fee. Not only will such cost accounting set up a remuneration fair to both client and agency, it prevents arguments and postmortems that could destroy the entire relationship. While one can safely advise agencies, particularly smaller ones, to work toward fee accounts for sufficient gross income, one must also add the hope that such work will not even be contemplated until the agency knows its costs and can prove them.

SCHEDULE OF BILLABLE HOURLY RATES

To let you bill a job on the basis of the hours put in on it, or to determine how large a fee should be to cover the work your people have put in, you must develop a schedule of hourly rates to be used for billing purposes. To give you the necessary income, your billable hourly rates must cover

- basic salary cost
- applicable overhead
- profit

In the examples I've used in the cost accounting section of this chapter, the agency's total overhead was $56,130 compared with

$47,810 of direct expenses. So overhead is 1.174 times direct expenses. Also, for the purpose of setting billable rates, you should aim for a profit of 20 percent (which means a markup of 25 percent on cost).

If you apply these factors to an employee whose salary is $32,000 a year, or $20 an hour on the standard 1,600-hour basis, you calculate his or her billable rate as follows:

Basic Salary Rate	$20.00
Applicable Overhead	23.48
Total Cost	$43.48
Profit	10.87
Billable Rate	$54.35

You would bill this person's time at $54.50 per hour. Since the factors to cover overhead and profit are the same for all employees, you could calculate all your billable rates by using a multiplier of 2.725 to convert basic salary rates to billable rates. To simplify the procedure, multiply the raw salary three to five times to arrive at the billable rate. This will give you some cushion, which is often sorely needed.

You can use a separate rate for each individual based on salary or you can set single rates for groups of people. For example, you might bill all account executives at $81.75 an hour, all artists at $54.50, and all writers at $68.25. This grouping method is the one I prefer because it disguises individual salaries.

Once you've established your rates, I recommend that you take the final step of converting them to a schedule or rate card. This should be made available to all clients and should be dated so it can be revised from time to time as conditions change.

— Part III —

Agency Finances and Ownership

—11—

How Do You Evaluate an Agency's Worth?

Evaluating the net worth of an agency is probably one of the most difficult tasks to accomplish. There is no inventory to sell and you're at the mercy of both a high labor turnover and the potential loss or gain of accounts. Past performance is one of the factors in determining net worth. However, you must temper it with current personnel, how long the accounts have been in the shop, and the potential of future earnings.

If you're interested in buying an existing agency, how much should you pay for it? If you bring two people into part ownership of your agency, should you give or sell them stock? If so, how much? If you are looking toward a merger, how can you tell what each agency is worth? A question closely related to all of these is, "What is a reasonable estimate of the minimum capital needed by an agency that has billings of about $5 million per year?"

HOW MUCH CAPITAL DO YOU NEED?

By answering the last question first, we can set the ground rules for all the others. So, let's assume the agency will have gross income of $1 million.

The typical agency would spend 57.0 percent to 67.7 percent of this on payroll, both direct and indirect. Let's say for our agency it is

63.4 percent or $634,000. It's also an old rule of thumb that it takes about three months from the time an idea is conceived, through production, billing, and all the other steps, until the agency gets the resulting income. So, you must be prepared to finance your payroll for this three-month period. This will require capital of $158,500. Also, there is furniture and equipment plus some work in process that can't be billed right now; so, this minimum capital should be increased to, say $200,000. There's one more complicating factor. If all your clients pay their bills on time (which means before you have to pay the media or other suppliers) all is well and good, but unfortunately clients delay payment. So, to be on the safe side, tack on another $50,000 in capital so that your normal capital, if you want to sleep nights, is $250,000, or 25 percent of your gross income.

TIMES EARNINGS BASIS OF VALUATION

So, the minimum value of our $5 million agency is $250,000 because that's what it has (or should have) in the bank. But anyone investing in an agency would want more than that—he or she would want future earning power to provide a return on the investment.

Normally you'd be willing to pay x times the agency's average profits, just as listed stocks are frequently quoted on a price/earnings ratio. A common rule of thumb has been that an agency's profit capability is worth from 5 to 10 times average after-tax profits. In the case of our hypothetical $5 million agency (or more properly $1 million business—see page 51) the gross profit before bonuses and profit sharing was $200,000, or 20 percent of gross income. After these two major distributions, the profit before taxes was $50,000, or 5 percent of gross income. If taxes were $7,500, that would leave a net profit of $42,500. On the old 5 to 10 times profit formula, the agency would be worth between $212,500 and $425,000.

Before adopting this approach, however, think a little about the nature of an advertising agency. It is a highly people-intensive business where physical assets have very little to do with its success. As Fairfax Cone once aptly remarked, it's the only business whose assets go down in the elevator every evening. This being the case, what makes the agency business succeed is what motivates its people, and this may bear very little relation to the bottom line.

For instance, I know several agencies that, because the total tax bite on the owners would be less, chose to operate under Subchapter S. In this case all earnings are paid to the owners as dividends or bonuses and they pay the taxes personally with the result that the agency corporation has no tax and no profit whatsoever. At the other extreme is an agency whose principal owner could not buy life insurance and whose principal aim was, consequently, to increase the value of his agency's stock as rapidly as possible.

Given these two admittedly extreme examples one can conclude only that an agency's net profit after taxes is an extremely weak basis on which to make a valuation. It is too subject to manipulation in the best sense of the word.

One way to adjust for this situation and still retain the times earnings valuation would be to adjust the agency's profit and loss figures to what they would be if it operated in a normal manner. This, it seems to me, is nothing but an exercise that can only raise questions as to what is normal and what adjustments should be made to reach the normal figure.

There is a great danger in relying on net profit as any kind of a base. One agency owner can draw a huge salary and thus drain the bottom line; another principal can take very little salary and show a very high net profit.

GROSS INCOME BASIS OF VALUATION

It seems much more logical to base a valuation on known facts, that is, the size of the business or its gross income and its net assets and leave it up to the purchaser to retain as much or as little profit as his or her preferred method of operation allows. This can, and probably will, bear no relationship to what the predecessor did. One rule of thumb relating future earning power to gross income has a maximum of 50 percent of a year's gross income. Numbers from 25 to 50 percent of gross income have been used in actual practice. If we assume a 16 percent factor, the earning power value of our hypothetical $1 million gross income agency would be $160,000. If you add to this the $250,000 the agency should have as capital, you arrive at a total value of $410,000, which is within the $212,500 to $425,000 range that results from using the 5 to 10 times profit basis.

So, no matter which approach is used, you come out just about the same. In either case, the particular point in the 5 to 10 times earnings range or the 0 percent to 50 percent of gross income range picked is based on a judgmental decision about the particular agency being considered.

While the valuation based on times earnings requires an adjustment of those earnings to what they would have been, given normal operations (whatever that means), the valuation based on gross income does not. Thus, it seems the latter is the sounder basis to use.

Pay As You Go

There's one more important consideration, however, that stems from the very nature of the agency business. This is the complete dependence of the agency's existence on the length of time clients are likely to stay with the shop. Tenure depends not only on agency efficiency or even creativity but may be affected by developments in the client's organization or industry that are entirely beyond the agency's control. The personality of the agency owner and the account executive is often vital to retaining business. The personal chemistry between new agency management and long-term clients may be such that clients become disenchanted and leave—and the new owner who thought he or she was buying a vital going business may find he or she paid good money for an agency rapidly going downhill.

So any payment for future earning power based on past performance may really be a huge question mark. How much more sensible for the purchaser (and beneficial tax-wise for the seller, also, if properly handled) to pay for future earning power only as it manifests itself over the years. A neat trick you say; how do you do that? Well, it's really very simple.

Let's extend our example one step further and assume that buyer and seller have both agreed that the price should be book value (or net assets or net worth) plus a premium for earning power of 16 percent of an average year's income.

Let's further assume that the payments for earning power will be stretched out over four years at the rate of 7 percent of the first year's gross income, plus 5 percent of the second year's, plus 3 percent of the third year's, plus 1 percent of the fourth year's. So, when the deal is concluded the buyer pays an amount equal to the agency's net assets, doing nothing more at this time than trading dollars. At the end of the first year he would make an additional payment equal to 7 percent of the gross income actually generated, and so on for each of the three remaining years.

For an illustration of just how this works let's go back to our hypothetical agency with billing of $5 million, gross income of $1 million, and net worth of $250,000. Let's also assume the 16 percent factor for future earning power. If the transaction were made at one time and based on past performance, the price would be 16 percent of $1 million or $160,000 plus $250,000 for net assets, or a total of $410,000. This could be a bargain or a calamity depending on whether the future earning power was actually there or not—that is, if the agency continued at the same level, started to grow, or started to decline. For instance:

Year	Factor Base	Static Agency	Growing Agency	Declining Agency
		Gross Income		
1986		$1,000,000	$1,000,000	$1,000,000
1987		1,000,000	1,125,000	875,000
1988		1,000,000	1,250,000	750,000
1989		1,000,000	1,375,000	625,000
1990		1,000,000	1,500,000	500,000
		Payment for Future Earnings		
1987	7%	$70,000	$78,750	$61,250
1988	5%	50,000	62,500	37,500
1989	3%	30,000	41,250	18,750
1990	1%	10,000	15,000	5,000
Payment for Earnings	16%	$160,000	$197,500	$122,500
Payment for Net Assets		$250,000	$250,000	$250,000
Total Cost		$410,000	$447,500	$372,500

A Phantom Premium

One final question remains: how this system could be adapted to the sale of a share of the agency to an employee and its later repurchase. Let's assume the employee wants to buy 10 percent of the agency and that it is in a static pattern during 1987 to 1990 when the stock is purchased. The total cost would be a $25,000 down payment plus an additional $16,000 over four years for the agreed share of future earning power. You collect the $25,000 down payment in cash but are reluctant to ask for further cash each year for many reasons, a principal one being that a typical young agency employee doesn't have much cash to spare. So, what do you do?

Well, you say, "We'll set up this premium for future earning power on our records and call it a *phantom premium;* then when you resell the stock to the agency, we'll calculate the sale premium on the same basis and deduct from it the phantom premium so you will get the book value plus the difference in the two premiums for future earning power." If, in our example the gross income for the years during which the agency is repurchasing stock is that shown in the second column, the employee would be entitled to a premium of 10 percent of $197,500, or $19,750. The actual cash receipts would be $25,000 at the time of the sale plus the net premium of $3,750 ($19,750–$16,000). This would be paid as soon as the total repurchase premium exceeded the $16,000 phantom premium. At the end of the third year the total repurchase premium would be 10 percent of $182,500 or $18,250 and the employee would receive $2,250 in that year plus an additional $1,500 the next year.

So, to sum it all up, there is no single method or formula for valuing an agency. The two major points that must be considered are (1) the agency's net assets and (2) its future earning power. Both of these factors may have to be adjusted to reflect the realities of a particular situation and they can be combined in an almost infinite number of ways. The figures shown above are only an example, albeit a realistic one, of how to evaluate an agency. This can give you a good idea of the size of the numbers you're talking about, but the actual valuation is a problem for experts.

DIFFERENT PRICES FOR DIFFERENT BUYERS?

In spite of the fact you might feel that, once established on whatever basis you prefer, the value of one agency should be the same for all potential purchasers, I believe that this is not the case, nor should it be.

At one extreme is the case of an agency that wants to buy your agency for any one of a number of reasons—to get a foothold in your territory, to expand its client list, or to acquire some top-notch advertising people. Whether this is called a merger as a face-saving circumlocution or is identified as the acquisition it really is, it is purely a business transaction. As such you should try to get the most advantageous deal you can.

In a transaction such as this you may use your formula valuation as a point of departure, but inevitably the final price will depend on the relative bargaining power of the two parties. How anxious is the other agency to get hold of your business, your clients, and your people? How willing are you to sell?

The factors you'll want to take into consideration will include guarantees on both sides, employment or consulting contracts, continuation of benefit programs, and terms of sale, to name a few—all highly technical areas in which you should employ expert financial and business advisers.

At the other extreme is the situation in which an employee or group of employees may want to buy an interest in the agency where they work. These are not strangers seeking to negotiate a purely commercial deal; they are, if you will, members of the family. As such you'll probably be inclined to give them more favorable consideration and terms than you would a stranger. An important factor is that these employees have been instrumental in bringing the agency up to its present value.

Then there's an in-between group—neither competitors seeking a takeover nor present associates looking for a piece of the action— but outsiders seeking a good investment. As such they'll probably be interested primarily in investment considerations such as earnings, dividends, growth, and stability.

In the next chapter I'll discuss some of the reasons employees or others might want to buy a piece of the business and why you might want to sell to them. We'll also consider some ways in which different prices might be determined for different groups.

—12—

Who Should Own
Agency Stock?

At the end of the last chapter I talked about employees and outsiders as potential owners of agency stock. Let's now look into this whole area more closely. A basic management principle states that if your company's goals match the individuals' personal goals, you have a better chance for success. That's why it's important to consider having your employees be part owners of your agency.

EMPLOYEES AS STOCKHOLDERS

Most agencies are started by one individual or at most a small group of principals. They own all the stock, though some shares may be put in their spouses' names for tax planning reasons. As the agency continues in business and, I hope, grows and prospers, it will add people, some of whom will become key employees whose activities have a definite effect on the success of the agency. At the same time the needs of the growing business may call for more capital than the present owners can, or care to, supply. So now comes the time to consider selling some stock. To whom?

Key Employees

Naturally you'll think first of your key employees. They help make the wheels go around. In earlier days they'd be taken into the firm or made partners, which is exactly what you're doing when you sell them some stock. You know them and they know you; what's probably more important is that they and your clients know each other. If all these relationships are friendly—and these associates wouldn't still be around, to say nothing of being key people, if they weren't—taking these people into the business can only strengthen the support on which the business is based.

Why would key employees want to buy agency stock? I can think of a number of reasons.

First, stock ownership is the ultimate form of profit sharing. If a person's efforts increase the agency's profits, and therefore the value of its stock, that individual participates in that increase to the extent of his or her degree of ownership. Thus, to a degree, one is in business for oneself and the master of one's own destiny.

Another benefit of stock ownership for key employees is to let them build for the future. Normally, for internal purposes, agency stock is shown at its book value, which is the smallest amount it is worth. On this basis, every time the agency earns a profit the book value goes up, and every time it pays out part of its profits as a dividend the book value goes down. As employees get financial reports month after month and year after year, they can watch their investment grow. What's more, they know that their own activities and decisions have a direct bearing on how their stock grows.

Other reasons why key employees would want to own some stock in the agency for which they work would be the boost to morale on becoming "a member of the family" and the right, as a stockholder, to receive financial reports to show how the company is doing. Generally speaking, these considerations are of secondary importance to the key employees, but they do have value to them.

Middle Management

Today's middle management people may be tomorrow's key people and perhaps future owners of the agency. To prepare for these more responsible roles they should acquire some familiarity with the corporate facts of life. What better way to expose them than to let them own some stock and thus be entitled to get reports and attend stockholders' meetings to see something of what goes on behind the scenes. At the same time you'll get a chance to size them up in this milieu.

These up-and-coming youngsters will also probably get a big boost in morale from being invited to become stockholders with the recognition that status implies. If you've appraised them correctly, you'll do well to tie them closely to the agency early in their careers.

There is also an inherent danger in bringing in minority shareholders. By law, you must reveal financial information to all shareholders, and you may not want to divulge salaries, perks, or other agency expenses. If you are prepared to share financial data, don't hesitate to offer stock to minority shareholders.

Other Employees

Sometimes stock is made available to other employees of lesser stature. Such shares usually are issued in small lots primarily to reward employees who have given the agency long and faithful service. They never can provide an important source of capital for the agency, but they can give big dividends in employee morale.

Employee Trusts

Agencies that have formal pension or profit-sharing trusts qualified under the Internal Revenue Code may be able to sell (or deposit as part of an annual contribution) some of their own stock to these trusts. I know of cases where this has been done but hasten to point out that such investment requires specific approval to corporations by the Internal Revenue Service, which will be given or refused depending on the circumstances in each case.

If you can get permission for the trust to make this investment, you'll reap several benefits. First, you'll be tapping a good source of capital for your agency and, what's more, one that won't want to withdraw its money unexpectedly.

Also, every employee who is a participant in the trust will automatically have a beneficial interest in the ownership of the agency. This can be a good morale builder.

So, if you have such a trust, or are thinking about establishing one, talk to your advisers about the possibility of the trust becoming a part owner of the business. This can play a big part in your agency's future.

How to Sell Stock to Employees

When you're talking about making stock available to employees, you are, in effect, taking them into partnership. Because of this special relationship, you'll undoubtedly make it as easy as possible for them to buy in. But remember well that word "buy." Don't make the mistake of giving them stock; they'll appreciate it much more if they have to pay for it. You may give them all sorts of help, but insist that they at least go through the motions of paying for the stock.

When you're thinking of selling stock to employees, your real interest is to reward outstanding performance, to tie key people more closely to the agency, to build a sound foundation for future growth. You're not trying to get the highest possible price for what you're selling. So how do you give the purchasing employee a break? Lots of ways.

Price. As I pointed out in Chapter 11, different kinds of purchasers of agency stock have different reasons for wanting to buy and you probably have different reasons for wanting to sell to each of them. Because selling stock to employees is one of the best ways to make your agency strong, you'll want to encourage employees to buy. Set the lowest price compatible with your basic valuation formula.

Payroll deductions. Many agencies selling modest amounts of stock to employees will let them pay for it by means of payroll deductions.

Bank loans. If the value of the stock sold is so large that realistic payroll deductions would stretch over too long a period, the agency can probably help by persuading its banker to lend the money to the employee backed by the stock as collateral. The agency can guarantee the loan, but the method I prefer, and which I have used successfully, is for the agency simply to guarantee the bank that it will repurchase any stock the bank may have to take over. In this way there's no actual or even contingent liability on the agency's books.

Bonuses. One common device is to give the employee a bonus (which she's probably earned anyway) with the understanding that she'll use whatever of it she has left after paying taxes on the bonus to buy stock in the agency. Or you can pay the bonus in the form of stock. In this latter case you'll probably have to include some cash for the employee to use to pay the tax on the bonus.

Repurchase Agreements

When you take an associate into the firm by selling him stock, you expect he's going to be with you for a good long time. In this highly mobile business, however, he could move to greener pastures at almost any time.

You certainly don't want an employee who leaves you for a competitor to continue to be one of the owners of your business. So, have a formal stock repurchase agreement that you have everyone sign when first becoming a stockholder. This should leave nothing to chance but should set forth explicitly the conditions under which you can repurchase the stock, the price to be paid for it, and other conditions.

As to price, some agreements call for one price if an employee quits, another if he gets fired, and still another if he retires or dies. Some even go so far as to repurchase it under some conditions at exactly what the employee paid for it. While there may be many reasons why you'd want to have an agreement of this kind, I think the fairest way for everyone—and hence for the agency in the long run—is to use the same basis for buying back as you used when you sold the stock. That is, if you sold it at book value, buy it back at its present book value; if you used a formula related to gross income when selling the stock, use the same formula (with the numbers updated) when you buy it back.

OUTSIDE STOCKHOLDERS

Once you get away from selling stock to your associates in the agency, you're bound to run up against a whole new set of values and priorities. Your business associates are advertising professionals who know how hazardous the agency business is, how slim its operating margins are, how dependent it is on the intangibles of personal skills and accumulated specialized experience, and how often accounts are lost as a result of someone's whim with no real fault on the part of the agency. They accept all this as an integral part of the business and, if they're really dedicated to their careers, want to be part owners of the business in spite of uncertainties and risks. They feel that their personal skills and contributions will go a long way toward overcoming the problems and making them masters of their own destiny.

Excluding an occasional rich uncle who wants to help you out, the only two groups of nonemployees who might be interested in buying agency stock are some of the agency's clients and the general public. Because the reasons for their wanting to buy and your wanting to sell are different in each case, let's look at them separately.

Clients

Other than getting money that may be needed to increase working capital, why would you consider a client as a purchaser of some of your agency's stock? One reason certainly might be to cement more tightly the agency-client relationship. After all, a client is a lot less likely to fire an agency of which he or she owns a piece.

Another reason might be a feeling on your part that you'd be doing business with a friend, quite possibly one of long standing, who knows something of the agency business and its rapid changes. As such, he or she would probably be much less likely to make waves if things slipped a little once in a while and might even make purchase of your stock on more favorable terms than a complete stranger would offer.

Why would the client be interested in buying your stock? The client may be buying it purely for its investment value, but that's not likely to be the principal reason. He is more apt to want to strengthen the agency-client relationship from his side so you won't be tempted to go after the account of one of his competitors. He may think he'll save some money by getting favored treatment from you or, at least, getting back some of his advertising expenditures by way of dividends on your stock.

"So," you may say, "there seem to be some pretty good reasons on both sides. Should we seriously consider letting a client become a stockholder?" My answer must be a resounding "no!" for this is starting on the road to becoming a house agency.

Do you want your client to know what your salary is? Do you want the client to start examining other salaries, time sheets, markup charges, billing rates, and any other information that may cause some problems? Do you want the client telling you how to run the agency? These are hard questions that need to be answered before you go ahead and offer stock to a client. The client can also intimidate you as a partial owner, asking for reduced rates, special favors, and other benefits to which he feels entitled.

What About House Agencies?

Because so much of the media will grant the agency commission to most any client or representative, a proliferation of house agencies has become much more common in today's advertising climate.

Every year AAAA publishes a report on house agencies—and every year the numbers seem to even out. In one recent year, there were 343 clients that fired their agency of record and went in-house. On the other side of the scale 421 clients dropped their house agencies and went back to an independent agency. Somewhere in this musical-chairs environment, there is an opportunity for you if you think beyond the normal parameters.

Let's take a look at some options:

- You can move your agency into a good client's office and become the house agency. There is some security, if that's what makes you more comfortable. All your costs will be covered: payroll, rent, utilities—everything. Then set up an arrangement whereby you can solicit and service other accounts and keep the profits generated from these accounts.

- You can offer to be the house agency and still maintain your own office location. This will guarantee a basic income each month and still give you a degree of freedom to do your own thing.

- You can work within a client's office one or two days a week and charge your normal consulting fee—and still carry on running your own agency.

- Or you may feel more comfortable in eliminating all the risks in running an agency and become a true in-house shop. All your creative, planning, and overhead costs are covered by the client. And that ain't all bad if you are inclined to play it safe.

If you think about your present situation and the client's needs, you may come up with some innovations that will serve your particular needs.

On the Other Hand

Let's look at it from the agency's point of view first. The minute an agency changes into a house agency, you as one of its principals stop working for yourself and become a mere employee. You're no longer master of your own fate. You can't take a flyer which, if successful, could be a gold mine for you but which would hurt no one but you if it flops. You've lost the profit motive.

On the creative side there would be none of the stimulus that comes from the cross-fertilization of ideas with people who are working in completely different areas. You'd miss the thrilling exposure to new advertising techniques devised originally for an industrial product, but which, with a little imagination, can be adapted to consumer products.

You'd lose the continuous exposure to a broad range of problems and hence, in time, a large part of your objectivity and even professionalism. You're bound to start losing your broad outlook and narrowing your horizons. Pretty soon you might be in danger of not being able to see the forest for the trees.

How about the advertiser who has his own house agency? After a while his advertising is bound to suffer from these same narrowing horizons and lack of cross-fertilization of ideas. His agency staff is always in danger of going stale with predictable and unfortunate results on advertising quality. If he becomes unhappy with a regular independent full-service agency, in the last resort he can fire that agency and hire a new one; this is almost impossible with a house agency.

The independent agency with a number of different clients can afford to keep a large staff with highly diversified skills because it can shift their efforts from a temporarily slack account to one that's at its peak of activity. It can call on the unique skills of an artist to solve a problem that may not come up again for a year for a particular client. Because that artist's skills are regularly in demand by a diversified list of clients, the agency can keep him busy as a key member of the staff. A house agency, with a single client, can't always do this.

Finally, how about the argument most often advanced for using a house agency, namely that the client firm will be able to keep for itself the profit the agency normally would make. I think this is a pretty weak argument because I doubt that the house agency can operate as efficiently as the independent agency with a much broader base of clients and products over which to spread its activities and its costs. Even assuming, for the sake of argument, equally efficient operation, the profit to be expected on an advertising expenditure of $1 million is only $83,000. This seems a very small amount for which to risk the success of the $1 million expenditure by using less than the most professional advertising people available.

Going Public

In recent years there has been a great deal of interest in agencies going public by offering some of their shares to the general public. As a matter of fact the first such offering was made in October 1929 by Albert Frank–Guenther Law, which sold a very small percentage of its shares. There was no further activity toward going public until September 1962 when Papert, Koenig, Lois sold about 20 percent of its shares to the public. Since then, many national and international agencies have sold shares to the public.

Benefits for the agency? Why would an agency want to sell stock to the public? There are many reasons, but the principal one has to be money. If you look into the public offerings you'll see that in almost every case the great bulk of the stock offered to the public has been sold by agency principals and not by the corporation. As a matter of fact, out of the public offerings for which data is available in *Standard & Poor's* or *Moody's,* 78.5 percent of the shares sold were for the account of stockholders and only 21.5 percent for the benefit of the agency itself. So, the motivation would seem to be to let the principal owners withdraw some of their investment in the agency. This is fine for the owners but does nothing for the agency itself.

There are expectations that going public will benefit the agency. Its liquidity might be enhanced by having its stock marketable; it might be easier to make desirable acquisitions if a publicly held stock can be offered.

Having its stock publicly traded might constitute recognition of the agency as being in the top ranks of the business, and the attendant publicity could bring the agency new business.

For the agency's employees, these same factors could be expected to increase morale and offer an incentive to greater effort. Their stake in the agency would be liquid and hence of greater value.

What the public wants. Why would members of the general public be interested in buying the stock of advertising agencies? Presumably for the same reasons they would make any investment. The yardsticks by which they would evaluate any company investment are, in approximate order of importance, (1) management efficiency and ability, (2) financial stability, (3) earnings and dividends, (4) the relationship between assets and liabilities, and (5) capital structure.

Simply by listing these we see how different the agency business is from most others. Let's examine each of them.

Of course, able management is important to an advertising agency, but in evaluating it, bear in mind that what makes an agency really tick is the quality of its creative product. This is not something that management can plan for as it can, for example, predict demand for a smaller automobile that it then proceeds to manufacture. Successful management in the agency business is the one that so manages its people and the conditions under which they work that the creative juices flow freely and the agency produces great advertising. This kind of management is hard to evaluate unless you are working in the agency day in and day out. As for financial stability, the largest agencies probably have it to a reasonable degree, but even they are subject to the vicissitudes of the business and the whims of clients.

I've talked before, particularly in Chapter 6, about the ability of the owners of an advertising agency to shift their own compensation, within rather broad limits, between salary, bonus, dividends, and appreciation in the value of their holdings of agency stock. This capability also extends to planning deliberately for zero profit in a given year to allow yourself to do other things—such as give extra rewards to key people— which will be much more beneficial to the agency in the long run.

As soon as you put stock in the hands of the public, you're bound to lose some of your freedom of action. Your outside stockholders will expect earnings and dividends regularly and won't appreciate that it may be in their best interest to forego earnings and dividends once in a while. As a matter of fact it's interesting to note that the president of one of the formerly publicly owned agencies, now in private ownership again, gave as one of the reasons for withdrawing from public ownership, the fact that he wanted to run the agency for the benefit of its employees rather than the stockholders.

As for assets and liabilities, an agency has no bricks and mortar, no machinery and equipment of any consequence, no patents, no valuable ownership of rights, no carefully constructed distribution system, no long-term contracts, and no exclusive privileges. Its only real assets— creativity, ideas, and talent—can't possibly be translated into balance sheet terms. On the contrary, most agencies operate in leased offices and have their names on long-term noncancellable leases that over a period of five years can add up to something approaching half their capital.

Under present accounting procedures these leases appear as notes to the financial statements and not as liabilities on the balance sheet. They could, however, pose a serious problem if things start to go bad.

Finally, capitalization. As I've pointed out, an agency is a people-intensive business rather than a capital-intensive one like a steel mill. This means that the amount of capital available for sale to the public is limited by the nature of the business. It's further limited by the desire of the principals to control the agency and thus their own destiny. A study of public offerings shows that, on the average, only 30 percent of an agency's shares were offered to the public and in no case as much as 43 percent. So, the public is bound to be a perpetual minority stockholder.

So, I must conclude that going public is a good device for the agency principal who, for whatever reason, wants to get all or part of his money out of the agency. It may have some benefits for the agency, but I think they are marginal at best and may be vastly outweighed by the erosion of employee morale and agency image if the stock declines in price in the face of what the agency people know to be highly successful operations.

I also can't help feeling that, while agency stock ownership is a tremendous benefit and incentive for agency employees, it is a reasonable investment for the general public so long as they stick to the size and quality of major players. For other, smaller agencies with a much more limited market, investment in agency stock is not recommended to the general public.

Perhaps the most important aspect of this whole question of outside participation in agency ownership is the effect it may have on what we now call "our public image."

We who are in the business know how hazardous it is. We know from sad experience that through no fault of our own we lose accounts we deserve. We know how narrow is our margin of operations, how difficult it is to show a profit. We're willing to take a chance, to work hard, and be so valuable to our clients that they will stay with us. Often this policy pays off. But suppose it doesn't and we have to explain matters to outsiders who have invested their money. Will they understand? You know that, as in any business, the many are condemned because of the failures or misbehaviors of the few. What if we add a money loss to their supply of complaints?

Think twice before you sell stock in your agency to outsiders. The main objection, as I see it, is the possibility of endangering our business standing, our priceless reputation for integrity. The risks we rightly take in our own shops can boomerang with fatal results if we let outsiders take them too. This prospect is a bummer for our business.

—13—

How Can You
Transfer Ownership?

It's never too soon to start thinking about transferring ownership. Most principals of small- and medium-size agencies say they're too caught up in running the agency, going after new business, collecting and receiving money, that they haven't the time nor the inclination to think about it.

Our advice? Think about it! There's nothing sadder than a "burnt out" agency president trying to have someone take over or trying to sell his agency.

Being natural optimists, the principals of advertising agencies expect that they'll live forever and see no point in thinking now about transferring the ownership and management of their agency to other hands at some time in the distant future.

The folly of this attitude can be demonstrated by the case of the medium-size agency owned by men I'll call simply John and Bill. This is a true story and I know the people involved but won't divulge names to prevent embarrassment. John and Bill each owned half of the agency, and everything was running smoothly until one afternoon Bill dropped dead in his office. A real shocker!

The agency's treasury bought Bill's stock from his estate and John became sole owner. This transaction went smoothly and all seemed well. Then John began to worry about his health, even to the point of believing he was in imminent danger of dying. For the first time he wondered, "Who's going to buy my stock? If we handle it the way we did Bill's, it'll take the agency's entire capital and there won't be that much cash anyway." He concluded he had only two choices— either liquidate the agency or seek an outside buyer. He chose the latter alternative, but his bargaining position was such that he got much less than he might have under better controlled conditions. How do you avoid this?

Plan Ahead Now

If you're willing to restrict yourself to the two choices with which John was faced, little planning is needed. If you go along with simple liquidation of the agency, all you need do is see that the assets are as liquid as possible and that they represent real and not wishful values.

The other option, sale to another agency, doesn't need much planning either. You'll undoubtedly get a more favorable deal if you sell your agency at a time when you can offer your personal active involvement for some period after the sale. This option calls for some planning, at least to the point where you set about doing it before illness or death forces someone else to do it for you.

The third option—and the one I believe most agency principals will want to adopt—is to have your agency continue operations, but under new management. This does require a lot of advance planning. The basic questions for which you're going to need answers are: (1) to whom should management responsibilities and control be transferred, (2) how and when should the transfer be accomplished, and (3) what device can be helpful in achieving this transfer?

Who Should Take Over?

Obviously the ideal purchasers are the people who can carry on the affairs of the agency with the least disruption and the greatest possibility of success. This means, of course, your present associates in the agency. They know the clients and their needs; they know the principles and philosophy on which the agency has been operating; they've devoted time and talent and effort to the agency; they've earned the chance to take over.

The key people in the agency, account executives and department heads, certainly should be included in the new ownership. If you believe, as I do, that a share in the ownership of an agency is one of the best and most widely appreciated ways of rewarding contributions to the agency's success, at the same time tying good people more closely to the agency, you'll want to consider extending the benefits of ownership beyond the key employee group.

Certainly consider the middle management group. They're likely to be the next generation of key employees, and by considering them now you'll be one jump ahead in planning for a future change of management. With the whole group—present key people and potential key people—consider apportioning shares in the ownership of the agency in relation to their contributions to its success. If you're foresighted you'll include some present evaluation of the future contributions of the junior members of the group.

How Do You Transfer Ownership?

Since most agencies are organized as corporations, the transfer of any part of the ownership is accomplished by the sale of shares of stock. So, what's complicated about that? Nothing until you come face to face with the fact that most agency people don't have a lot of ready cash with which to buy stock. What's needed is a stock purchase plan to allow employees to buy stock on terms they can afford. Here are some methods for achieving this.

Payroll Purchase Plan

With this arrangement, you tell the employee who's buying stock that you'll accept payment over a period of months by making regular deductions from his or her paychecks. Of course you must have a cash down payment from him or her and you'll need a signed agreement to cover the monthly deductions. This kind of plan puts you in the banking business, which is not your forte, so you'll want to put pretty strict limits on how far you go. Generally, I think any payments for stock purchased under a payroll deduction plan should be completed within a year.

Bank Loan Plan

If the amount involved in the purchase of a block of stock is larger than you can, or want to, handle on a payroll deduction basis, consider working out with your bank a program under which it will advance the necessary funds. Of course, it will probably want some assurance from you before making the loan.

You could guarantee the loan to the bank or even cosign the note, but this puts at least contingent liabilities on your books that you may not want. Another way is to tell the bank that if it accepts your agency's stock as collateral for the loan to the employee—which it would do anyway—the agency will guarantee to buy from the bank any shares it may have to take over in case of default. In this way, you're really utilizing the agency's credit to help the employees buy stock, but as long as everything goes as you hope it will, no liability appears on the agency's books.

Low-Priced Stock

Another device some agencies have used is to create a second class of stock. This new stock has a very low value, but at the proper time it can be given control of the agency by converting the original stock, which the principals continue to own, into a preferred stock to be retired out of earnings on some mutually agreeable basis. There are many ways of doing this, including the use of a voting trust, but the details can get pretty complicated; so be sure to consult expert advisers before starting a program like this.

Employee Stock Ownership Plan (ESOP)

This kind of trust is a variation of the stock bonus trust that was first recognized in the tax code in 1921. Little was heard of it, however, until it received special recognition and favorable tax treatment in a series of tax laws enacted in 1973–75.

An ESOP is a trust, qualified under the Internal Revenue Code, whose principal purpose is to use before-tax dollars contributed to the trust by the agency for the purpose of buying agency stock for later distribution to employees. The stock can be purchased from retiring principal owners or from the agency's treasury. This lets the ESOP become a device for transferring agency ownership from retiring principals to second generation management, or it can be used to raise additional capital to finance agency growth.

Like everything else, an ESOP is not the answer to every agency's problems under all circumstances. There are limitations and conditions surrounding its use that may make it undesirable for many agencies. But, in the right circumstances, it can be a lifesaver.

When you're talking with your expert advisers—accountants, lawyers, and bankers, to name just a few—about plans for raising capital or for the eventual transfer of ownership of the agency, by all means ask them to look into an ESOP and its application to your particular circumstances.

OTHER THINGS TO CONSIDER IN YOUR PLAN

Once you've decided on a basic plan you'll want to look into some features that may be helpful in some cases.

Buy-Sell Agreement

If the agency is owned by a small group of principals, it would be wise to work out between them a buy-sell agreement. This would set forth just what happens to the stock of each principal if he or she should die, retire, or simply leave the agency. You'll want to be specific about whether the agency or the other principals buy(s) the stock. Be sure to establish how the price is to be set and how the stock is to be apportioned among the purchasers. You can make any provisions you want, but the important thing is to work the program out well in advance.

Insurance

Many agencies use life insurance on the principals as a means of funding a buy-sell agreement. These policies can be owned and the premiums paid by the agency itself or by the other principals. Of course, every case is different, but it's certainly something you'll want to look into; and don't forget the tax consequences of the different ways of handling the insurance.

Consultation Contracts

Many, if not most, principals won't want to cut all ties to the agency when they retire. The agency probably wouldn't want that either, nor would the clients who've been relying on the principal's advice for many years. One way to ease the transition is to write a contract for consultation by the retiring principal so you can call on him as needed in future years. This keeps him interested, gives the agency the benefit of his experience, and can go a long way toward solving the financial problems that can arise for both agency and principal at retirement time.

Gradual Phasing Out

One plan I've seen in operation calls for a gradual progression toward full retirement, beginning five years before the anticipated retirement date. During the first year, the principal sells a fifth of his stock in the agency and takes a two-month vacation; the second year he sells another fifth of his stock and increases his vacation to three months. This goes on until, at the end of the fifth year, all his stock has been redeemed and he has gradually increased his time off to such an extent that it's but a short step to full retirement. During the five-year period it would be quite reasonable to make reductions in salary as vacation time increases.

This kind of plan has the advantage for the retiring principal of making a gradual shift from full participation to none, as regards agency ownership, working time, and income. For the agency it has the advantage of knowing when stock is to be repurchased, and how much, and being able to plan to meet the changes in personnel requirements. It seems to me to make more sense than to go serenely on until retirement day and then *whammo!*

You Can Never Start Early Enough

Plan *now* for the transfer of ownership to avoid real problems when the time comes, and when, realistically, you may not be around to help work them out. The specific steps I described briefly are only a few of the approaches you'll want to think about.

Every situation is different—different people, clients, financial situation, business climate, and desires on the part of the principals. These specifics were mentioned only to give you a basis for your own thinking and discussion with your advisers. It's important to remember that with plans as complicated as these you must have the best professional advice you can get. This is no field for do-it-yourself projects. The point is, each of these devices has worked, and worked well, for one agency or another. Maybe one of them is just what you want.

But plan ahead! Don't wait! Do it today!

It bears repeating: Now is the time to think about transferring ownership of the agency. It's like going after new business: you're so busy running the agency, you have no time for new business. So it is with long-range change-of-ownership planning—you never seem to find the time.

I hope these suggestions will give you an incentive to start this project in motion.

— Part IV —

Agency Organization and Operations

—14—

The Care and Feeding
of Employees

Research studies of new business presentations indicate that one of the most important factors in choosing an agency is the chemistry between the agency people and the client. That's why there never was a business so highly personal as advertising. It depends for success on individual work, inspiration, and enthusiasm. It makes use of temperamental, imaginative, highly strung individuals to whom a word of praise in the proper spot can mean far more than money. So the selection, training, and handling of your people is about the most important thing you can do to ensure success.

How Do You Locate and
Select Employees?

How do you pick those rare individuals who can help an agency for the long range. For example, an agency is expanding and needs additional personnel. It defines its requirements precisely; it probes the applicants' samples and checks their references; it uses psychological tests, but with only moderate success. Apart from all these methods for finding good employees, are there any additional techniques or approaches?

From the reference to samples, the agency is apparently seeking to fill a creative job, but the general principles to be used in recruiting for any job are the same. The differences between selecting people to fill one job or another will be basically differences in the emphasis given one factor or another.

What Are You Really Looking For?

First, it is advisable to define clearly the kind of people you want in your agency, all the way down the line, and refuse to hire anyone who does not meet these specifications. You want loyalty, balance, humanity, realism, the willingness to work, a self-starting discipline, compatibility, and, of course, intellectual honesty.

Second, set down in full detail the responsibilities of the job you are seeking to fill. In the case of the creative person being sought in the above example, just what is expected and on what terms? Do you want independent writers and planners or people who work best in creative groups or under the guidance of a copy chief? Must they do contact in addition to their creative duties? In brief, just exactly what is the job?

Third, add to your list of basic traits you seek in all employees some others that would be particularly applicable to the specific job you are filling. These might include ability, knowledge, experience, and attitude, all of them defined in terms of the specific job.

What Do You Have to Offer?

Before seeking new people, you should look carefully at your own situation. What makes your shop a desirable place to work? Why should any able advertising person prefer your agency, compared with others offering practically the same money? Without this plus, you will have difficulty in attracting the type of people you want—ambitious, able, and loyal. Set your standards high, but to attract this sort of personnel you must come out on top when rated by these same standards yourself.

So, let's see what makes an agency a good place to work.

Realistically, money is the first consideration. Not necessarily only the amount, but also the manner of earning and receiving. While good advertising people may not want to make financial sacrifices to join an agency, they will be favorably inclined toward any agency that makes them feel they deserve the money they get and their remuneration bears a direct relationship to the money the agency is making on them. This brings us to the ways of rewarding people, which will be discussed in a later section of this chapter.

The second element that makes an agency a good place to work is appreciation. Creative people particularly need this. They simply cannot work efficiently and happily without enthusiastic recognition of their talent. As an agency owner planning to take on creative personnel, you must look at yourself sharply and realistically. How good an employer are you? How well can you understand and sympathize with the idiosyncrasies of others? Are you tolerant? Do you have the intuitive appreciation of the creative process?

Maintain an exciting creative climate and be lavish in your recognition of creativity. When I was an account executive, every time I returned to the agency after showing a client our creative product, the creative people would literally bombard me with questions like "How did they like it?" "What was the client's reaction?" Creative people need to know how their work is accepted and whether it was approved by the client.

Returning to the original inquiry of this section, the answer may well be, "If you want people of the high caliber you outline, it is not enough to put them through all the fitness tests. Subject yourself to the same analysis, or one even more rigorous. How well have you held on to your present personnel? How long have good people stayed with you? When you lost some, was it your fault or theirs?"

A great responsibility rests on any employer who has in his hands the happiness and peace of mind of even a few employees. He has no right to hope they are happy. It is his duty to see that they are, because his is a position of power.

Where Do You Look for People?

Well, of course, you have access to all the regular sources such as employment agencies. There are even some of these, mainly in New York and Chicago, that specialize in advertising people. Then there are the classified ads in newspapers and in the advertising press—*Advertising Age* and regional publications. Another resource is your local Ad Club. Most cities of any size have an Ad Club and often an Art Directors Club or other specialized groups. If you belong to an agency network, the executive secretary may know of available people. Other possible sources are the many colleges that offer courses in advertising. Most of them keep lists of their graduates and many stand ready to help them find the kind of jobs they want. Make contact with the placement offices of these schools.

The agency business is a volatile one because advertisers change agencies with often distressing frequency, agency people shift from one shop to another, and agencies merge or, on occasion, split apart. What's more, all this is made highly visible by regular listing of such changes in the national and regional advertising publications, the daily advertising columns that appear in many metropolitan newspapers, and in bulletins from the *Standard Directory of Advertising Agencies.*

From all these published sources you may get a pretty good idea of available people. Most agency principals, however, when faced with the necessity of reducing staff because of lost accounts or mergers are eager to help their people find new jobs. So, inquire around and you may help them while helping yourself.

EDUCATING YOUR PEOPLE

Questions on how much agency people should know, before and after being hired, how to pick the right employees and then make them better, how much time can profitably be spent on education compared with that used in the more obvious agency activities are much more important than they seem on the surface.

Too often sight is lost of the fact that a business depending on the abilities of individuals, glibly called a service business, must give better and better service to survive. It's not enough to worry about the end product of marketing and advertising advice and its implementation in the form of plans and copy. Agencies succeed in direct proportion to the abilities of their people.

So it would be well, I think, if agency heads wondered occasionally if continuing attention to education such as the medical professions demand might not be advisable and profitable for our business.

What is the too-frequent agency image of today, as seen by the advertisers? Cleverness, the ability to make a fast buck, superficiality, irresponsibility? Wouldn't agencies be better off if they were thought of as staffed by responsible, well-educated, soundly based individuals who think before they speak? Certainly if agencies want the latter image, they need the personnel to build better agencies. They need educated people who know that education never stops, and it's our responsibility to help them continue learning all through their business lives.

One East Coast agency I know took an unusual approach to this problem. It set up an internship program that recruited students from local colleges to work in the agency under the dual supervision of the

agency's account executives and the college faculty. They
with overall responsibility for research, creative ideas, ...
mechanicals, and other such duties. The first group of three, ...
graphics designer, and a writer/producer, got straight A's for enthusias...
effort, and performance. When the program ended, the graphics designer
became a permanent member of the agency staff, one of the others went
to a New York agency, and the third set about writing plays. The agency
considers the experiment a success. An internship program can provide
a great source of fresh talent. Bright, enthusiastic advertising and marketing majors can supply much-needed backup help for modest costs.

Once you've found and employed the kind of desirable people
you're seeking, you should begin to educate them in agency techniques
and procedures and keep on doing so. Instead of letting your people
spend their time adding up figures, clipping tear sheets, writing to
someone else's specifications, or drawing along preprinted lines, see that
they know why they are doing what they are doing, and what it means
in the final agency product.

Work hard and constantly, you agency owners and managers, to
sell your people on the need to know more, to be of greater potential value to your clients. Resist the notion that new ideas are better
than good ideas. Get the whole shop sold on the theory that we are
in a reputable business, that our customers trust us to advise them
soundly, that we succeed only as we help our clients succeed, along
sound and constructive lines. Discourage opportunism, snap judgments, and fast footwork. Encourage honesty and hard work. Always
give more than the client expects.

Don't expect your people to stay overtime to be educated. Teach
them on company time, not on theirs.

To summarize: Get the right people with the right educational
background. Keep on educating them by practical experience, case histories, and talks by executives who know what they are talking about.

When you, or your people—or any of us for that matter—stop
learning, we are on the way out.

How Do You Compensate Your People?

"Simple," you say, "you pay them." Well, of course that's true, but that's
not the whole story because there are many ways of paying people.

Also, different kinds of compensation may have more or less appeal for different people depending on their age, health, family status, and other considerations. What appeals most to Joe today may be a lot less attractive a few years from now after his kids are educated and he begins to consider the possibility of retirement. So let's look at the different forms compensation can take.

Salary

The basic consideration in setting an employee's salary must be what he or she is contributing to each of the functions the agency must perform. The guidelines given in Chapter 5 can be a real help in the evaluation of responsibilities. To show how this can work, let's assume that Pat, an account executive, is responsible for two accounts that together bring in $200,000 out of the $1 million of total agency income. The amounts available for salaries for the various functions might look like this:

Client	ABC	XYZ
Gross Income	$120,000	$80,000
Contact (approximately 19%)	22,800	15,200
Creative (approximately 16%)	19,200	12,800
Implemental (approximately 11%)	13,200	8,800

In addition, 11 percent of the $1 million total agency income would be allotted to general administration and new business. That is $110,000.

Let's also assume that Pat does 75 percent of the contact on ABC and 50 percent of the XYZ contact; 20 percent of ABC creative; 17 percent of XYZ implemental (buying media); and 10 percent of the agency's administration and new business.

This can be put together to give us a rough approximation of what the agency can afford to pay for the things Pat does.

Contact	75% of ABC	$17,100	
	50% of XYZ	7,600	$24,700
Creative	20% of ABC		3,840
Implemental	17% of XYZ		1,496
General and Administrative	10% of Total		11,000
			$41,036

So, as a point of departure in considering Pat's salary, you would be in the area of $41,000. This should be checked against the going rates in your city and especially those paid by local agencies comparable to yours. You can't afford to get too far out of line.

Another important consideration is what salary Pat feels she would need to make her a happy, productive member of your team. If you feel she has real potential to become, in time, a part owner of your agency you may want to go a little higher to hold her. When talking compensation with people of high caliber and promise, be sure to discuss the whole compensation picture with them—not salary alone, but other benefits, especially profit sharing and possible future participation in the ownership of the business.

Salary or Commission?

You may well ask, "If you can come up with an approximate salary for an account executive by applying your basic guideline percentages, why not go all the way and pay her totally by a commission based on these guidelines?"

You can do this, of course, and many agencies do. Arrangements for a split of gross income between agency and account executive are fairly common.

For many reasons I don't like this way of compensating account executives. On purely philosophical grounds I dislike the implication that the accounts a person handles are personal accounts and the executive is simply using the agency's supporting services. This may be true, at least initially, but to accept this premise puts the agency in a vulnerable position. If the accounts really belong to this person, he or she can take them and go elsewhere whenever he or she wants, to the agency's detriment.

I think you should adopt the far better philosophy that all accounts are *agency* accounts—and then do everything you can to make that a reality. Make sure the client sees more agency people than just the account executive; make sure he or she is aware of the contributions made by all of your people. Another danger of paying on commission only is that you are setting up the climate in which each account executive is concerned only about pleasing his or her own accounts and doesn't concern himself or herself about the rest of the business in the house. You must set up a team effort in order for the agency to be successful.

On a more practical note, you can't run an agency by feeding numbers into a computer. The percentages I've been talking about are very useful as guidelines, but that's all they are. Every agency is different, so adjustments always have to be made; what's more, the situation in any single agency is continually changing, and what may be true today may be dead wrong six months from now.

Another practical problem is that these guidelines are designed to cover functions, so if an account executive needs help in contacting his client, the cost of that help has to come out of the percentage of income allotted to the contact function. You can't dock an employee's income just because the principal goes along on a few client calls, and you surely can't tell the owner he can't go. But the value of the principal's time must come out of the contact allotment. So you can see how this system will probably result in questions about who's doing what on an account, how much he's doing, and whether it's really necessary.

About all that can be said in favor of this way of paying account executives is that it is better than remuneration based solely on comparative bargaining power. At least it has some foundation in fact and is a formula an agency can follow with assurance of not going broke.

Reward for New Business?

Isn't it fairly common to reward an employee who brings in a new account by paying him or her a commission based on the gross income from the new account? Yes, it is, but I feel it's subject to all the objections discussed above. There's also the added complication of deciding who is really responsible for getting a new account. It's very rare that only one person can be credited with bringing in a new account. What if the principal goes along for the presentation?

If you can get around the problem of who is entitled to what part of the credit for landing a new account, some financial reward may be appropriate. One method of new business compensation that has been used by agencies is paying the account executive who brought in the account 2 percent of the gross income for the first year. This could be dangerous! As one agency principal reported, "I've had account executives rush into my office asking for a bonus right after they acquired a new account. But I've never had anyone come into my office and ask for a salary reduction after losing the account." Another way to reward bringing in a new account is to make a single lump sum payment with the amount set in reasonable relation to the size of the account.

I believe, however, that the best way to reward an employee's contribution to new business is to make the results of that activity one of the things you consider when you're making a periodic employee evaluation. Thus, new business activities can, and should, be an important part of an overall evaluation and salary adjustment.

How About Bonuses?

There are two kinds of bonuses that are widely used. One is the year-end bonus, usually a relatively small amount distributed to all employees on a uniform formula as a sort of Christmas present. There's no real problem here except that you should keep reminding your people that this is a bonus and not part of their regular salary. If you don't do this, you may have a full-scale crisis on your hands in a bad year when you can't make any extra payment.

The other kind of bonus is the purely discretionary one used to reward selected people for outstanding individual performances. The thing to watch out for here is that payment of such bonuses may become a habit—and an expanding habit at that—that employees come to expect. So, make it truly a reward for unusually valuable individual performance. Don't distribute such bonuses to most of your staff, but single out the top performers. Don't pay bonuses to the same employee year after year; if he's that consistently an outstanding performer, his salary should be increased.

An effective technique is the surprise bonus—nothing will put a shot of adrenaline into the agency's morale more than unexpected cash. It works wonders! But, once again, be wary of setting up an expected, regular bonus. When you can't deliver, it can really backfire on you. Employees have been known to be so disgruntled that they threw negative shock waves throughout the agency and even quit.

Pensions and Profit Sharing

These are the two most common forms of retirement plans. As such they are an important part of your total compensation package. While there are any number of informal plans called by one or the other of these names, what I'm writing about here are formal plans approved by the Internal Revenue Service and designed to provide deferred benefits for the participants. It is a feature of all these plans that payments into them are not taxable when they are made, but only later when withdrawals start.

In return for these tax benefits, the IRS has set up very strict rules and regulations as to what you can and can't do. Since the rules are changed from time to time it is very important that you consult your attorney and your auditor before establishing one of these plans or making any changes in an existing plan.

The fundamental difference between the two types of plans is that the pension plan provides fixed dollar benefits and imposes fixed costs on the agency that must be paid whether the agency earns a profit or not. It is basically an actuarial proposition, that is, a strictly mathematical calculation based on age, length of service, and salary.

The profit-sharing plan, on the other hand, provides a proportionate share in the total fund that has been built up. There's no compulsion on the agency to make a contribution unless it has profits to share. The agency's contribution can be based on a formula, or it can be largely discretionary. Such a plan won't become a burdensome obligation in a poor year and will let you make up for lost time in a good year.

A sound profit-sharing plan should let employees participate on a basis that recognizes their length of service and the value of their contribution as measured by their salaries. Any number of systems using points to measure these two factors can be used to tailor a plan to your own shop and its people within reasonable limits. You might, for example, give one point for each year of service and one point for each thousand dollars of annual salary. Or you can change the point schedule to give more weight to either service or salary as befits your particular situation.

I am a wholehearted advocate of profit sharing as a vital part in an agency's plan for compensating its people. Its growth from year to year lets a key employee see some direct results from his or her own efforts on behalf of the agency.

Share in Ownership

To invite a key employee who's shown the ability and loyalty to become a part owner of the business is the ultimate degree of profit sharing. But it's a lot more than that. It's making your employee a member of the family; it's saying loud and clear for all to hear, "Here's a person in whom we have confidence and who is going places." It takes him out of the employee category and transforms him into one of the partners—a person who's in business for himself.

Fringe Benefits

This category covers a large group of programs an agency may offer to some or all of its people. One of the most common is an insurance package that may include any or all kinds of protection for the employee—life insurance, hospital and medical protection for self and family members, disability income insurance, and other new coverages that are being dreamed up all of the time. This kind of insurance usually is bought on a group basis at a more favorable rate than the employee could obtain individually. The agency may pay the whole cost or share it with the employee.

Some agencies, if business needs warrant, may make automobiles or club memberships or the use of recreational facilities available to some employees. Some agencies have been known to lend a valued employee part of the down payment on a house or arrange bank credit for him or her.

Fringe benefits will appeal differently to every employee. The agency that uses them imaginatively and tries to tailor them to individual cases will be rewarded by increased employee loyalty and morale, and reduced turnover.

HOLDING ON TO YOUR PEOPLE

Agency people are of more than average intelligence and drive; they're usually creative, fairly highly strung, somewhat emotional, and certainly sensitive. You have only to look at any issue of *Advertising Age* to know that they're highly mobile. Sometimes they're lured by the glamour of one of the major advertising centers, sometimes by what seem to be greener pastures in a competing agency in your own city. So, how do you hold on to a good employee in whom you have a large investment of time and money?

Sensitive Treatment

Failure on the part of the principal to treat his account executives sensitively is probably the cause of most resignations. It usually results from the power that inherently belongs to the agency head, for no doubt about it, power is one of the most difficult things for humans to handle. Unless you are acutely aware of this, unless you sense the fear and uncertainty that besets the person you've hired, and whom you can fire if you feel like it, you're looking for trouble.

Adequate Compensation

No doubt about it, people are held best by a proper remuneration program properly administered. This covers all the forms of compensation discussed earlier in this chapter. An adequate salary is probably the strongest single tie binding your people to your agency in almost all cases. So make sure that your salary levels are competitive.

In other cases, however, salary alone is not enough. The time comes when certain individuals stand out from the crowd by virtue of their abilities. These people will be held and kept happy only by a share in the agency's ownership, with all the prestige (as well as the difficulties) that this involves. But note one thing. The agency owners must sense this need and meet it before the individual begins to show dissatisfaction. If the pressure comes from the employee, the ownership transfer is tainted. The relationship is hurt. "I had to put a gun to his head before I got it!" remarked one good man who recently acquired a piece of an agency. How long do you think he will remain in this shop?

Be sure you make the sharing in ownership a real one. It must include a sharing of the real responsibility and true authority.

Publicize Your Benefits

It's just human nature to take for granted something that keeps on coming in month after month and year after year. This is particularly true of your employee benefit programs, which are designed to be there when people need them (as in the case of insurance programs) or which continue to build up values for the benefit of the employee at some distant retirement date.

So, tell your people what you're doing for them; tell them how much it's costing you; tell them what it'd cost them to go out and buy these programs on their own. Don't be bashful. You're paying out a pile of cash for these programs, and you don't get any benefit from them unless your people know what you're doing for them and appreciate it.

In the nineties, health-care packages have become extremely expensive, and most employees welcome a good plan that protects themselves and their families. Don't let your employees take this added benefit for granted. Have periodic staff meetings and discuss the benefits . . . health plans, profit sharing, bonuses, whatever you are offering.

How About Restrictive Agreements?

Many agencies ask their key people to sign agreements, in consideration of their employment, that they won't go into competition with the agency for a period of time after they leave its employ. The agreement probably also will provide that they can't work on the account of any agency client for the same period. It's not an easy matter to draft such a document that will stand up in court, but it can be done, and I know agencies that have collected damages under such agreements.

While you probably should ask all your key people to sign noncompetition agreements as a matter of good business practice, don't count on them heavily to help hold your people. Because the agency business is so highly personal, no legal document can make an unhappy employee stay with you. And if he's unhappy, you probably wouldn't be happy with the work he's doing for you anyway.

Some agencies require a noncompete clause that prohibits employees from taking accounts away from the agency. Such contracts can act as a deterrent and have been fairly successful in most cases. But realistically, all such an agreement can be expected to do is get you some monetary compensation if employees steal accounts. But against this you'll have to weigh the time you'll have to spend, the legal fees you'll incur, and the publicity you'll create if you decide to go to court. How much better it would be to work hard to make all your accounts *agency* accounts so no one employee could take them with him even if he tried. This seems to be the way to build a sound and long-lasting agency business.

—15—

How to Be a Good Account Executive

There's an old adage in the agency business that seems to hold true: "If you listen to the client long enough, he'll write the copy for you." This doesn't mean that you do exactly what the client wants; it means that the client is telling the account executive what he wants to get across about the product. It's the account executive's job to interpret the information, distill it, and provide the most creative approach on how to sell the idea.

In any client-agency relationship the contact function is the hyphen; it is the interface that enables the two organizations to work together; it is the conduit through which information is transmitted from client to agency or from agency to client. In the eyes of the client the agency contact people are the agency; to the agency staff the contact people speak for the client.

In the agency scheme of things the contact function serves three main purposes—to see that the client's business is handled properly, professionally, and efficiently; to see that the agency retains, or better yet increases, the business; and to see that the agency handles the business at a profit.

Many accounts have been lost, not by creative, production, or improper billing, but by the kind of relationship that exists between the client and the agency's account executive. The account executive represents the agency; his role is to keep the client happy and to persuade the client to want to continue to do business with the agency.

GUIDELINES FOR HANDLING THE CLIENT'S ACCOUNT

It seems pretty obvious that if the contact people don't handle the client's business properly, there soon won't be any business to handle. So, it's important to review what it takes to handle an account properly.

Understanding

As one Texas advertiser put it in a seminar attended by agency people, "It is essential that the agency understand the client and its business; what it has to sell and how it sells it; the way the client thinks; its internal policies, problems, and bottlenecks; the pressures of time on top client advertising personnel." This is a primary responsibility of the agency's contact people.

Only by steady contact with everyone concerned with the client's promotional activities can the agency learn about all phases of the client's business. Don't forget that the client has been at this all his business life; yet we come in and are expected to advise him authoritatively on matters that may have troubled him for years.

All the information and rapport we can accumulate will be little enough to save us from bad breaks and make our advice worth listening to. Only personal contact can give us this real feel of a business. If we don't get it, we stay in the dark and our marketing recommendations are correspondingly limited or downright incorrect.

But we must go far beyond surface knowledge of a business and try to enter into the hopes, aspirations, and ideals of the people who run it. This sympathetic understanding of clients is of the utmost importance.

Build a Partnership Relation

The contact group should strive to build a true partnership relation with the client where agency and client keep each other fully informed and where unpleasant surprises seldom arise. This kind of attitude, which arises from steady contact, makes the agency a true partner in the client's success, with a priceless inside knowledge of the details of his or her business. A client is slow to fire an agency that has acquired this feel for his or her business.

An agency that has achieved this partnership relation should not become complacent. Just as if it were employed by the client as sales manager, it should constantly be looking for trouble spots, trying to improve what may seem to be a satisfactory situation.

The more an agency has become an insider in the advertiser's business, the better chance it has to hold on to the account. Consider for a moment how an agency account executive may become so familiar with his accounts, on such terms of personal friendship with the advertiser's people, that he is able to move the account from agency to agency. This is an example of the power of being too close—and it is also a hint to keep both the contact man and the account happy, so as not to be confronted with this unhappy development.

Build a Comprehensive Plan

The agency, spearheaded by its contact people, and the client must work out a comprehensive marketing plan to achieve the client's goals. The plan should spell out the objectives to be reached and the ways of doing so. It should demonstrate creative thinking by the agency in conducting a successful search for the uncommon solution to a common problem.

The plan should provide for periodic review of results with the client to determine whether the advertising has been effective. The measure to be applied here is not whether the advertising has won a hatful of awards (however pleasant and flattering to the ego of the creative people that may be) nor even whether the client is enthusiastic about it. The true measure should be whether the advertising has achieved its real purpose—to sell what the client wants to sell.

Who Should Contact Whom?

Smart agencies, I think, are those that spread the contact chores around so that people in one organization get to know their counterparts in the other. The account executive is primarily responsible for client contact and will probably do the great bulk of it personally, but it's a good idea once in a while to take along some of the troops who are doing the detail work—a writer or artist or media person, depending on need. Take the principal along once in a while, too.

On the client's side, contact by the agency should go further than just the top people in the client's organization. It's fine to have the owner pleased with us. But it's equally important to sell everyone else down the line who has anything to say about the company's promotion work or who is affected by it.

Particularly important are the sales manager and his or her salespeople. All advertising and sales promotion efforts should obviously
be channeled through and coordinated with the sales department.

Technical Follow-Through

The agency can't handle the client's advertising properly without
competent follow-up throughout the shop. By this I mean the professional, workmanlike performance of all the steps needed to implement
the advertising plan—production, media buying, estimating, and
billing, to name just a few. As the agency's chief point of contact
with the client, the one who gets egg on the face when something
goes wrong, the account executive must be responsible for seeing that
the agency performs all of these implemental functions properly and
on time.

The Contact Report

The contact report (or conference report or call report), that simple,
obvious, essential detail of good agency practice, is not in proper use
by one agency out of ten.

What is meant by "proper use"? Here are a few questions and
answers that may be illuminating:

- *Who writes the contact report?* Usually, it's the account executive
  who is handling the account.

- *When is it written?* The same day as the conversation takes place
  or the instructions are received, if this is possible. People forget mighty fast.

- *What are its contents?* Generally, the three elements of a contact report are the *subject* (what's the project we are talking
  about?), the *discussion* (what information do we need?), and the
  action plan (what are we going to do to follow up on the
  assignment and who from the agency is responsible?).

- *Who gets copies of the contact report?* Everyone in the agency who
  is concerned with the activity recorded, and everyone in the
  client's organization who is similarly interested. In this way, each
  person who is responsible for a specific function knows what
  he's responsible for.

- *What happens to these copies?* They should be carefully filed, preferably in loose-leaf books under each client's name, with a file cross-indexed by decisions.

- *Do you need a contact report when the price or the decision has already been covered in some other written form, such as an order or a letter?* Yes. Let there be one place where all these vital decisions are regularly recorded. Otherwise they will be scattered so widely that you never can find them when you need them most.

With properly kept records, even years later it should be possible to reconstruct every campaign, every step in every agency job, together with who authorized what and, if possible, why.

The factors that make it so difficult to maintain complete records of all contacts and decisions are, of course, pressure of other jobs, procrastination, the feeling that memoranda and letters are all that are needed, and plain laziness.

Among the benefits of well-kept contact reports are preventing protracted postmortem arguments with the client, the coordination of all concerned in both the client's and the agency's organizations, and the instant availability of relevant facts in emergencies, or when some individual is sick or on vacation and someone else has to pinch-hit.

There are some less obvious benefits, too. Contact reports circulated among all those in the agency interested in this particular client may well result in constructive suggestions, often from the least-expected sources. That is if such suggestions are invited, as of course they should be. Nobody has a monopoly on ideas.

Also, in the give and take of the agency-client relationship, too many decisions are made off the top of the head by all parties. Contact reports confirming the course of action contemplated give us the chance for a second look, and avoid the misunderstandings that so often wreck an otherwise delightful relationship.

So the contact report is not simply something that is good to have if you can take time for it. It is the agency's most reliable protection against forgetfulness, change of personnel, or undeserved blame for someone else's wrong decisions. With the large sums of money involved in today's advertising operations, with the dangers to the agency's survival that may result from misunderstandings, the contact report is of fundamental importance. Of course, if you already have a workplace computer system, you can E-mail the contact report to the client and send copies to all those associates involved with the job.

CONTACT'S ROLE IN
HOLDING CLIENTS

Frequent client contact by agency people of standing and authority is a vital essential for holding and expanding business.

As any rancher can tell you, keeping your fences mended is the best way to prevent cattle from escaping. Business jumps from one agency to another for one or more of three main reasons: client dissatisfaction, justified or not; promises of more for their money from competing agencies; and some form of conflict or other difficulty between the agency and client.

The first two are the ones the agency needs to know about in time to take measures to improve the situation. The ability to smell smoke is a great agency asset. Big changes spring from the small beginnings of a little discontent, perhaps with our charges or the way our secretary talks over the phone. Sitting in the client's lap, as a California friend expresses it, is a vantage point from which to recognize and correct immediately any little vexation that may soon assume alarming proportions. Only contact, frequent, never perfunctory, and with the right people in the client's organization, makes rapport possible.

It isn't enough to sell our clients. We have to keep them sold. If we don't, someone else will.

Don't forget that a client with whom we sit down today may have just met with a competitor of ours, not because he contemplates a change, you understand, but because it is his duty to his company to learn as much as possible about other available agency services.

Frequent personal contacts not only spread the mortar of friendship between the stones of your relationship, they enable the agency to be selling itself constantly, which it must do, considering how many other agencies are waving special inducements under the client's nose.

It's tempting to say that agencies hold business by rendering good service; yet, while the production of effective advertising for clients is an essential for holding business, it is by no means the only one. Sadly enough, we all know of cases in which agencies have lost accounts on which they have done excellent jobs. This was because of changes in the advertiser's organization, unexpected developments within the advertiser's own field not anticipated by the agency, and policy shifts, desirable or otherwise. Competitive solicitations by other agencies also cause many account changes, especially where better deals are offered, financially or with longer credit terms.

Definitely, to have the best possible chance to hang on to desirable business, the agency must add constant attention to the client to its good service program.

Finally, we need to remember that agency service, and indeed advertising itself, is constantly on trial in the mind of the client who pays the bills. It calls forth an entirely different attitude from that enjoyed by other expenditures for more concrete or more easily evaluated commodities or services. This state of mind is something to be combatted constantly, not only by superlative service but also by physical contact on a regular basis, scheduled in advance and augmented by special calls whenever required.

The more frequently the agency sits down and thrashes out problems that confront the advertiser, not only those of advertising, but also those of all marketing, of which advertising is a part, the more uncertainty fades and certainty and reassurance grow.

HANDLING AN ACCOUNT AT A PROFIT

Advertising agencies are in business to make a profit and should not be reticent about it. Clients don't object to their agencies' making a reasonable profit; in fact they expect them to be good enough businesspeople so they will earn a profit. If you come across a client who doesn't feel this way, watch out!

As the person most involved in all phases of the agency-client relationship, the contact person is the one properly charged with so handling the account that the agency comes out with a profit. How does one do it? By adopting the right attitudes and backing these up by actions consistent with those attitudes.

Be Money-Minded

From the very beginning of the relationship let the client know that you are concerned with money matters. Start right out by discussing fully and frankly what you bill for and how. Be specific.

The fatal procedure is to start on an account with a vague and generalized understanding on both sides of how the agency will be compensated and then try to fix things up later when the agency wakes up to the fact that it is losing money on the operation. This is, of course, due to the human reluctance to face facts or to talk money during the delicate days of the honeymoon. Don't fall into this trap!

When talking about a specific job, go beyond what has to be done to do it right and mentally figure what it's going to cost the agency to do it. Maybe there's an equally effective way that will cost the agency less.

Try to inculcate this money-mindedness into all your associates in the agency. It's only human nature for a dedicated creative person to want to keep on redoing an advertisement in search of perfection. Aside from the fact that there is no such thing as true perfection, you should indoctrinate your people with the economic facts of life, and in particular the law of diminishing returns.

Be Businesslike

By this possibly enigmatic statement, I mean never undertake a job unless both agency and client clearly understand what is to be done, who is to do it, and what the costs are to be. In other words there should be an initial estimate. This should provide for adjustments in case the ground rules are changed part way through the job. It should be clearly understood, for example, that once an advertisement has been approved by the client, any changes to be made in it will be charged for in addition to the original estimate.

Another way to manifest a businesslike attitude is to avoid making off-the-cuff promises that you may or may not be able to keep. When a client asks if final production on an ad can be completed by Friday, don't just say, "sure." How much better to say something like, "I'm sure we can, but I can't promise until I talk to my production people."

Then you can call the client the next day and say, "Yes, we can meet that deadline with no strain," or, maybe, "We can do it, but it'll take several hundred dollars' worth of overtime."

This situation brings us to the last businesslike action I'm going to discuss. This is to be sure, whenever there's a change in an estimate for a job, particularly an increase in cost, to get written confirmation. Maybe a simple conference report or a revision order will suffice, but be sure to have something. It may be some time before the job gets billed and human memory can be short. Why take a chance on arguments and ruffled feelings when a simple businesslike procedure can avoid it?

Some Emotional and Psychological Considerations

Of individuals it is often said, "We get back from the world just about what we give it." This is another way of saying that each person's attitude toward life strongly influences his success or failure. Without a doubt, the agency's attitude toward its clients is as influential in holding or losing business as its creative ability. Attitude is expressed in the manner, the matter, and the frequency of contacts.

There is a strong emotional element in the agency-client relationship of which sensitive advertising people are acutely aware. It is almost like a marriage. Yet you always have against you the fact that no matter how you phrase it, you are an outsider looking in. You are not a part of the client's organization, on its payroll, rising or falling with its successes or failures. You have other business on your books. If the client fails, you will survive.

These are the emotional background feelings of which you must be aware. As much as possible, you must eliminate them and substitute for them the feelings characteristic of the ideal employer-employee relationship. Literally, you must become, to the greatest possible extent, a member of the client's company.

The reason so many advertising accounts follow one individual from agency to agency is not, as so often believed, that person's familiarity with the client's business. It is almost invariably the fact that the person in question has established with the client this personal trust, this emotional relationship. As the client so often puts it, "He speaks our language," or "He's really a member of the family, not just a business associate." This is definitely emotional, and you never want to underestimate the power of emotion in our business.

There's an important corollary to this. If individuals in the agency establish an emotional relationship with the client, thereby becoming influential in holding the business, the agency should establish the same sort of relationship with these individuals so it will be sure to hold on to their services.

When I talk about establishing an emotional relationship with the client, I'm talking about developing a true personal understanding. This is an understanding by the agency person of the basic forces behind the advertiser's activities. What really makes him or her tick?

Why is he or she spending this money for advertising? Is it only to facilitate and increase sales? Or are other ambitions and aims involved? Frequently the client is entirely unconscious of these hidden urges. But the more the agency person understands them, the more helpful he or she can be, and the more likely to continue the relationship.

Such an understanding by an account executive expresses itself in a sympathy and warmth of which the client is instantly aware. If he or she put these feelings into words, they would be, "This is more than a business relationship. He wants my account, and he wants to work with me, not only because of the money he will make in the process, but also because he is interested in what I am trying to accomplish."

I hasten to say that I'm not advising you to simulate this empathy. In the first place, this is something you are unlikely to be able to fake. In the second place, insincerity once detected is strong poison. No, this attitude, this desire to team up with the hidden motives of others, provided they are worthy ones, is one of the strongest of all feelings that holds human beings together only when it is genuine. It goes not only for agency-client relationships, but for all business and personal contacts in life.

Remember, too, that while honest advice is essential, so is horse sense. There are bound to be times when advice is resented and angrily resisted. The client has a psychological problem of his or her own, often one inherent in power. A person in a position of authority, especially on the spending of large sums of money, may well be sensitive about his or her prerogatives. One does not gratuitously step on this person's toes.

Never say to a client, no matter what the provocation, "Well, we have a few other jobs to do, you know." All very true but, to the client, his or her account is the only one in your shop. If you don't make him or her feel that you are operating as if this were the case, watch out for trouble.

HOW TO BE A GOOD ACCOUNT EXECUTIVE

- Keep in step with clients
  - Make them look good to their management.
  - Become indispensable.

- Initiate ideas and suggestions rather than just take orders.
- Don't be subservient.
- Be firm when you are right.
- Provide the best possible advertising service.
- Always give clients more than they expect
  - Anticipate problems.
  - Go out of your way to beat a deadline.
  - Stay ahead of clients.
  - Plan and present programs they don't expect.
- At agency-client meetings, listen first—talk later
  - You can't have an answer until you've heard the question.
- Become indispensable to your clients
  - Take care of things that are a chore for them.
  - Make recommendations and suggestions long before clients begin to think of them.
  - If they have a decision to make, get clients in the habit of calling you for advice.
  - When you become indispensable, you control the account.
- Always prepare an agenda
  - Keep clients on track—when they wander, get them back on track.
- Prepare a conference report
  - For each subject list discussion, action to be taken, and who is responsible for taking action.
  - Assign responsibility for action to your staff.
- The best source of new business? Your present clients—make a friend, make a sale.

SOME BASIC POINTS YOU MAY WANT TO REVIEW WITH YOUR ACCOUNT EXECUTIVES

- Know the clients' product or service.
- Let clients know what their competition is doing.

- Keep constant contact.
- Read the advertising press and the clients' trade journals.
- Prepare call reports after every meeting.
- Keep your clients' information confidential.
- Always proofread everything that goes out.
- Keep existing clients apart.
- Always be prepared for client meetings.
- Always have clients initial new copy, new ads, press releases, etc.
- Be a good listener.
- Don't go over budget.

Conference Report
Your Company Name
Address
Telephone number Fax number

Client:
Date:
Place:
Prepared by:

Present for Client:
Present for Agency:
Copies to:

Basic Subject: New fall campaign

Subject	Discussion/Action	Responsibility
1. Advertising schedule	1. Budget to be determined as well as list of publications.	1. Gene to obtain rates, deadlines, etc.
2. Ads for publications A. Display B. Classified	2. Layout copy, approach to be determined.	2. Creative department to prepare
3. Public relations campaign	3. Need announcement for straight releases.	3. Bob to write, Gene to edit
4. Publishing of articles	4. Series of three prepared by Bob.	4. Gene to edit
5. Label for audio cassettes	5. Copy to be determined.	5. To be discussed (Gene has draft from Bob)
6. Direct mail campaign	6. To be test-marketed.	6. To be discussed with Creative

—16—

It Ain't Creative Unless
It Sells

In order for creativity to be effective, it must sell the benefits of the product or service. What are you looking for? A good feeling about the product? In direct response media you are looking for direct response, whether it's by coupon, order form, an 800 number, or a Web site address.

The latest research indicates that consumers are bombarded with five hundred to a thousand messages a day. As they wake up to the clock radio with its accompanying commercials, they continue to be exposed to morning TV, the daily newspaper, billboards on the way to work, and so on through the day, until they finally fall asleep, exhausted, while watching a late movie.

It's really tough for an advertisement to get noticed—and remembered.

Creativity is that indefinable aura or substance that is truly the heart and soul of an advertising agency. All agencies claim to have it, but when the TV commercial instantly grabs the viewer, when the convincing idea jumps off the page and makes an impact on the reader, the creative function has delivered its promise.

Before any copy is prepared for any media, the message must carry the big "B"—the Benefit to the reader, viewer, or listener. The prospect mentally is asking, "What benefit do I receive from buying and trying this product or service? Will it save me money? Will it make me pretty?

Will it improve my income?" If there is no benefit, there's no point in listening to the commercial or reading any more of the ad.

Many times shock value is used to get attention. The consumer may remember the ad but probably will not remember the name of the product.

CREATIVITY IS THE HEART
OF THE MESSAGE

The creative function covers a lot of territory. It embraces the complete expression of the promotional plan in words, pictures, or anything else that can convey the message.

One major component of the whole creative package is art in all its forms—computerized layout, comprehensive, finished art, photography.

Another is copy, from the few simple words needed to convey the message to a motorist passing a billboard at 65 m.p.h. to a full page of solid copy explaining a complicated proposition. Don't forget, either, the completely different problems in combining selling and some entertainment in a television commercial that may last only thirty seconds or less.

Television also requires a liberal dash of the theatrical, including the proper selection of actors, decisions as to lighting, music, and the like. Most of these activities are left to the studio actually producing the film or tape, but the agency must be capable of supervising so it can be sure the final product is right. This broadcast production responsibility is usually included in the agency's overall creative function. In addition, this department is usually charged with supervising the business aspects of television such as assuring that the right prints or tapes are sent to the right stations and that proper payments are made to the talent.

Point-of-purchase materials make up another important part of the whole promotional package. Sometimes a separate department is set up to handle everything connected with these materials, but more frequently they are assigned to the regular agency departments including, of course, the creative.

Occasionally an agency will become involved in such activities as the design of a new package or even a logotype for a client. It then becomes part of a highly specialized design function and usually charges a special fee for this service.

Now that I've outlined the extent of the area covered by the creative function, let's get down to some specifics.

GUIDELINES FOR WRITING
EFFECTIVE COPY

As the saying goes, "different strokes for different folks"—and so it goes with writing copy. Each medium has a different climate, a different environment that requires the most effective approach for that specific audience that is tuned in or reading your message.

Here are some basic principles to follow when writing copy for the different media. These are merely highlights to help you become familiar with each medium and its characteristics.

Television Commercials

The most important point is to grab the viewer's attention. It's been researched and reported that the first five seconds of a commercial are crucial to the success of the message; from then on factors like registering the name of the product, setting a tone, selling only one idea, and reaching your audience take over. Do you want them to buy your product; to be more aware; to call an 800 number?

Print Advertising

How do you read an ad? Research shows that 80 percent of the readers never get past the headline. Photographs are usually more effective than drawings. Talk in terms of the readers' interest, not your client's. For action, use an 800 number or include a coupon.

Radio

You have only ten, thirty, or sixty seconds, so sell one idea and don't clutter up the commercial with many features. Radio is timely; make your commercial newsy and take advantage of the format of the station . . . "golden oldies," "rock," or "country." Listeners are tuning in to these stations because of their musical preference, so match your message to their audience.

Outdoor and Transit

Again, we're looking for the one big idea that will register quickly and dramatically. Use large letters, and usually no more than seven words on the board. Billboards offer an excellent opportunity to show dramatic design, color, photography, and impact.

Direct Mail

The most effective use of direct mail can be made by testing. You send out partial mailings with different approaches, then see which approach pulled best. In some cases, long copy has proven to be effective: make your copy work hard and ask for action.

RESEARCH WILL HELP YOU

Listen to the consumer. Talk to people who use your client's product and to those who don't. In each case, find out why. Quite possibly, the search for a product story may indicate the need for a change in the product itself, its price, or its manner of distribution. No use telling your story well unless it's a good one. What consumers want to know is, "What's in it for me?"

If the product is selling well against competition, there are definite reasons for its success. These are the facts that belong in its advertising—all of them. The best advertising tells the product's story as well as, or better than, the product tells it. What people want from advertising is information, and often they get too darned little of it.

If you look straight at copy creativity, you will not even begin to write until you are convinced that good copy will sell the product. If you are in any doubt about that because of the product's own character, stop, look, and listen. No amount of advertising, no matter how good, will sell a poor product. You may, and probably will, get initial sales. Without repeats, however, these cannot build a business.

The ideal advertising to offer your client is based on a foundation of research and marketing facts. Once you have constructed this foundation, it is permissible, and indeed desirable, to implement your knowledge with brilliance, provided always that this does not depart from selling fundamentals.

Good ideas are sound, simple, easily remembered, true and honest, and attuned to the consumer's predilections. If they are also unusual, striking, and ingenious, well and good. These three, however, are secondary requirements compared with the basic five.

DEVELOP THE PROPER ATTITUDE

In the development of an advertising program both client and agency are shooting for something unusual, something sure-fire, and something new, a reliable stimulus that will interest an audience and make it take action. To this endeavor the agency's creative staff brings its skills as expert consultants, specialists in advertising communications. The client brings a desire for increased sales and profits and also an abiding interest in the qualities of its product or service.

This combination of factors can, at times, result in some pretty substantial emotional involvements. So it's important that from the very beginning the agency's creative people adopt the proper attitude to the client, the product, and the consumer. Toward the client they should adopt the attitude of complete frankness and honesty. They must always be true, if you will, to their own intellectual integrity and steadfastly avoid creating advertising designed purely to please the client.

The agency must chart the course of the advertising program, put on the brakes fast if anything seems likely to get out of control, and insist on solid foundations before building superstructures. It must resolve firmly to advise the client as to his or her best interest.

Regarding the client's product or service, you, as a writer, must know your subject. By this I mean not only understand it in every aspect, but feel it, be in sympathy with it, and be possessed with a burning desire to extol its virtues. If what you're writing about doesn't seem to be of surpassing importance to you, you won't write anything important about it. Writers can write fluently about almost anything. They write convincingly, however (and this is advertising), only about something in which they believe. They can't fool themselves or their readers. What's more, if they are honest, they will admit it.

Regarding the potential user you are seeking to convince, your attitude must be one of interest and sympathy. What is he like? What is his background? What are his capacities? His weaknesses? His prejudices? His knowledge? How intelligent is he? And finally, to what favorable or unfavorable influences has he already been subjected in the area you are pursuing? Is it, so far as your case is concerned, virgin territory? Or is he already preconditioned for or against you?

You must be willing to put yourself in the shoes of the consumer. Like an orator or actor, you can sway your audience only if you identify yourself with it—in short, become your audience at the moment of creativity.

Use the Line of Least Resistance

For every product or service there is one best way to sell it. This is the line of least resistance to the selected user's mind, supposedly discovered by analyzing what that product does for that consumer. Somewhere there is a common ground on which the product you are selling and the people to whom you sell it meet. When you find that, a good part of your work is done. The rest is craftsmanship.

In essence, great copy involves a preconceived correct selling slant and expresses it in the one absolutely best manner to get into the reader's head (and his heart) with the maximum impact and staying power. This means that even if you are a great writer you must know your subject. The most polished, terse, compact, beautifully expressed collection of words is just so much puff unless it says something. Too often magnificent writing is this and this alone.

There is one best way to say what you have to say. You may hit it first crack out of the box, especially if you have written at white heat. Such a performance may need only some polishing, some refinement. It was right to begin with and the less you fuss with it, the better.

Most of us, however, write many versions before the best one takes shape. Once you've done the job as well as you can, set it aside for a while if you have the time. Then review it and either decide that it's right on the nose or scrap it and start over. Remember, too, there are few pieces of writing, no matter how good, that cannot be improved by condensation. There are many ways, long and short, to express a thought. Can you say it better in fewer words? Fine! But don't cut merely for the sake of cutting.

Beware the trap of seeking attention for its own sake. The common-sense way to attack such problems as these is to ask yourself, when considering any procedure or selling strategy, one fundamental question: "What final mental result am I shooting for?" Not what *first* mental result, but what *final* mental result. Please note the important distinction. Not just attention, which any salesperson can get by standing on his head in the prospect's office, but conviction and desired final action. If this question were asked on every projected selling or advertising campaign, we would save our clients large bundles of money.

This sort of thing is much harder to sell to clients. What they want is something different—attention getters. I know that; I've been sitting across from clients for quite a while. I know what they buy most easily. But that's not the answer, is it? So, you may say, how come you see so little great advertising? Once every couple of months, if you read advertising constantly, you encounter great copy. Not much oftener, I'm afraid. Well, how often do you encounter a great painting, an outstanding play, or a top piece of musical composition? Why should it surprise us that great advertising is just as rare? It is of comparable difficulty.

MANAGING THE CREATIVE FUNCTION

In the preceding section I talked about the need for a sound foundation on which to base a creative effort, the need to develop a proper attitude, and the importance of finding the one best way to tell the story. Once you've instilled in your people this basic philosophical approach to creating good advertising, how do you, as agency principal, go about trying to ensure that your agency's output will have that spark of superior creativity that distinguishes the really successful agency from the merely adequate one?

Top Management's Responsibility

You should continually assess and evaluate your agency's performance in creativity. Is it doing merely an honest and workmanlike job of promotion complete with a sincere interest in the client's welfare but with little creative spark? Or is there real creativity? What do I mean by that?

I think that greatness in all of the communications arts—literature, music, sculpture, painting, and advertising—has one single characteristic. It is the injection of life into matter previously dead or dormant. Without this, the communication soon dies; with it, it lives. So, continually review the agency's output and ask yourself, "Is it alive?" Even if you can't write great copy yourself, you can recognize it when you see it, give valuable help to the creator, keep the feet on the ground while the head is in the clouds. Manage all you want to see that the sales message and all the other musts are included, but don't mess with the words if they sing.

Keep the Client's Hands Off

Once a piece of great copy has been written it must be steered past the client with its inspiration intact, which brings us to the whole subject of client involvement with creativity. He pays the bills and sees no reason why he should not contribute his best judgment to the finished creative product. "You know advertising," he says, "and we know our particular business. If we both contribute what we know best, the final product should be as effective as possible."

This may sound fine but, far more often than not, it just won't work. Take a lesson from lawyers and doctors. When you hire one of those to keep you out of jail or the hospital, you don't tell them how to do it. You put the responsibility where it belongs, on the guy who is supposed to know the answers.

To an almost equal degree, the responsibility for top creative thinking should rest with the agency. The client's function is to be sure the ideas suggested are realistic, that they do not conflict with facts that the client knows more about than the agency. Advertisers should not set themselves up as authorities on copy, art, media selection, or any other functions that are part of agency creative work.

As early as possible in the relationship with your clients you should clearly establish that the agency is the expert advertising practitioner. Properly and tactfully approached, clients are glad to find agencies that want to take on the entire responsibility for how and where and when the advertiser's money is spent. They have much more respect for the agency that knows its business and does not hesitate to say so. Agencies have failed to land accounts for many and varied reasons, but I have yet to hear of a solicitation that failed because the agency had the courage of its convictions. You don't have to be cocky about it. You have to recognize that there are definite factual areas in which the advertiser must be consulted. Say this at the outset, so you won't seem to be assuming knowledge you do not possess. But when it comes to creation, this is where you know the answers, and the less your suggestions are interfered with the better the results will be.

So, have the courage of your convictions. If you feel that the creative work is exactly right—not just fairly good or calculated to please—submit it to the client and be prepared to fight for it. By all means avoid the all-too-common error of showing the client several different versions for his choice. Set the agency up as the creative expert, and stick to your guns!

How About Quality Control?

As the advertising agency grows in size and the principals can no longer be involved personally in all the planning and execution of creative activities, it becomes necessary to develop some central supervisory body of executives who will periodically review the agency's operations and make recommendations concerning them. It is best to keep this group as small as possible; the more people you have on it the more difficult it is to get them together, and the more chance conflicting opinions will arise.

This body is usually called a "plans board" and consists of the agency principals and the top creative thinkers. To serve on such a board is an honor and a recognition of the fact that the individual is an important factor in the agency's success.

It is desirable to decide in advance just how wide a scope the plans board should encompass. In some agencies this committee reviews copy, supervising the creative output only. In others, especially the larger shops, the plans board may well watch all the agency activities: contact, research, internal functioning, new business activities, and so on.

Usually the plans board functions as an advisory body only. It makes recommendations to individuals or departments within the agency. To operate properly the board must meet at some preset time every week or, at least, every other week.

The operation of a plans board is based on the principle that creative work, the agency's only exclusive asset, is too important and valuable a commodity to be entrusted to any one individual, no matter how able. The plans board acts as a safeguard, and in the overall work of the agency, the final decisions are those of the committee, which represents the agency. Once this fundamental principle is understood and accepted by all concerned, the way is clear to an agency operation that ensures that the client receives the best possible service.

Principles of Pretesting

With advertising being such an intangible influence and one almost impossible to measure in most cases, I can't imagine why any good advertising person would fail to test the creative product in advance whenever possible.

If facts are available, fine, but in the many instances where uncertainty prevails, you're better off to pretest. This is commonly called copy testing, although it usually goes beyond this to include all types of advance experimentation with appeals and methods of promotion.

Probably a lot more copy testing would be done were it not for the misunderstanding these words create. Too often we think tests will give us facts, when these actually are not obtainable. We expect testing to do the impossible, instead of being thankful for any indications it may give us of the right road.

Principle 1: Don't expect the impossible.

Principle 2: Try to test only one thing at a time. It is surprising how often this rule is broken. Where more than one factor is at work (such as headline and body copy, or headline and picture), it is impossible to segregate one from the other and determine which is doing the job. Thus, when testing the comparative effectiveness of two advertisements, in split runs, let us say, let them be exactly alike in all respects except one—the heading or the body copy or the picture.

This maintenance of uniformity in all but one respect also holds for time of insertion and size of space. Don't compare advertisements run in July and January, when seasonal factors may be operating. (And they are often powerful in ways you easily may overlook.) By the same token, never try to compare advertisements of differing sizes—you can't.

Principle 3: Beware of laboratory tests. These fool many of us. They are easy, tempting, and usually deceptive. Laboratory tests include all opinion tests with such questions as, "Which of these advertisements do you like best?" The question may be asked of an office associate or a nationwide consumer jury. The laboratory method is somewhat more reliable when we use coupons and costs per inquiry to indicate the comparative power of various advertisements. But this still indicates that we are foggy in our thinking as to what we are trying to find out. If you want to know how many people will send for a free cookbook, that's one thing. But it proves nothing about how many people will respond to this particular selling slant and buy your product off the shelves.

Principle 4: Determine if it is often practicable and economically desirable to test small at first. Especially as we adhere to our rule of testing only one factor at a time, we need to seek small space (less than one-eighth of a newspaper page) rather than large for our comparisons.

We have to be careful, however, that our small space insertions do not become invalid when we eventually use larger space. This, of course, is a matter of judgment and horse sense. To achieve true testing you must use the same size ad in the test and in the actual campaign.

How about pretesting television commercials? Will these principles permit realistic testing of this important form of advertising?

It is extremely doubtful. Elaborate theater showings of commercials are often conducted before audiences to find out what is liked and what is disliked. Some general indications may be the result. Again, however, how close are the conditions of this test to the actual conditions under which the commercial would be viewed at home? What will buying reactions be in the supermarket? Will consumers behave in stores as they do in your theater? One fears that many other factors are present in real life that cannot be duplicated in laboratory tests.

—17—

The Follow-Through—
Getting the Job Through
Production and Traffic

Consider traffic as you would a road trip; starting from one destination and ending at the final destination. Production is the element needed to complete that movement. After the account executive meets with the client and gets the assignment, many steps have to be taken to make sure the job is completed, on time, within budget, and with no costly errors.

Since this book is concerned primarily with agency management, it can't go into detail on those many highly specialized functions that ensure that the advertising message, once created, actually appears. Some of these occur before, some during, and others after the creative process. Without them, the advertisement can't possibly appear at the right time, in the right place, and in the right physical form.

The agency principal can't be an expert in all these fields, but he or she should be familiar with the basic functions in order to evaluate the job of those entrusted with the day-to-day operations of the departments involved.

Here is a brief description of what I've called implemental functions, with some of the basic areas each should cover.

MARKETING

The term *marketing* is often used in a broad sense covering business activities far beyond those that normally belong under this term. Just what is marketing? Marketing is moving a product or service from conception to consumption, with growth and profit. The word "moving" is the key to this definition. Any activity that contributes to that movement is marketing. Anything else may be called planning, research and development, budgeting, or something else. The movement to which I refer takes place through definite channels of distribution, with the help of skilled individuals in various parts of the distribution chain.

A good agency should be intensely interested in marketing. It should know exactly what its client is doing to facilitate this movement. It should be able to spot what is weak and emphasize what is strong. If only for its own self-protection, since its advertising is designed to help sales, it must be sure nothing interferes with the implementation of its plans and delivery of its promotional message. The agency has to help keep the channels clear and the merchandise flowing. Motion is of the essence.

Two basic principles are crucial to the success of selling a product:

- The product must be a good product. It's so obvious, but it's basic. Products that don't deliver the promise may have a meteoric start but never get to the finish line. Customers simply will not come back for repeat sales. So, before you advertise your client's product, make sure it's saleable and will perform for the customer.

- You must have effective distribution. No product has ever succeeded without a good distribution channel. Whether it's through distributors, wholesalers, discount stores, or mail order, customers have to know where and how to get their hands on the product.

The Agency's Responsibility

The agency owes it to itself and its client to do all it can to ensure that its plans and creative work are not stepping up to the plate with two strikes on them. This may call for a lot of homework and even some fieldwork before you touch that computer. Is the product or service right? Have you satisfied yourself that the product or service you're being asked to advertise fills a need or desire of the user? Is it attractive? Is it priced right?

If the product is normally sold through stores, it's not too difficult or expensive to run a practical test. Set up a sort of retail laboratory using maybe a half-dozen outlets strategically located in various parts of the country, plus a special cash inducement to compensate the store owners for having their shops used as a proving ground. This is the age of discounts and coupons, which should be part of every test.

Now, with the advertiser's approval, you can work on evolving a selling formula originating at the point of sale in which the two basic marketing elements operate in proper sequence. You may need point-of-sale material, demonstrators, or other measures. This process will let you discover under real-life conditions whether the product is desirable and what happens when it is available under favorable circumstances.

The least that can happen after such an experiment is an improved picture of the product's character, and trade attitudes and consumer reactions to it.

How about availability? There's no better way to create ill will than to have a potential customer come into a store all set to try out a new product that he or she has seen advertised only to be told, "We don't have it in yet. Come back next week." The moral, of course, is don't let your client advertise until the product is available in the area where it's being advertised. The old belief that advertising creates distribution doesn't always work; it's putting the cart before the horse.

The best advice, probably, is to make haste slowly. Consolidate your position before advancing. Testing is vital!

Once you have a favorable selling effort in your test areas you can expand your market to the whole of the test areas and then to the surrounding regions. You will be constantly monitoring how your advertising plays in various markets and ensuring that adequate product is available to meet the demand you have created.

Go national only when local territories have been adequately exploited, and be sure you leave enough promotion money in them to retain the success you have won.

Go national only after wide enough distribution has been obtained to ensure against customer disappointment.

Go national only when accurate figures show that this way you can now sell for less money than (or equal money to) the local market in terms of the relationship of total promotional expense to sales.

How do you learn these things? There are lots of sources. Start with data on distribution your client's sales department has gathered. Then check surveys available from the media. Many of them regularly make store checks in their own areas and will be glad to give you the information. Some of them will make special spot checks for you.

Then there's always specially commissioned research. You'll most likely want to retain an outside research organization for studies in motivation—what customers think of a product, what makes it desirable—and market research to check on distribution and dealer attitudes.

Who pays for this? There's more on this subject in the research section later in this chapter, but the basic rule should be this: If the research is for the education of the agency to help it produce better advertising, no charge to the client; if it's for the client's benefit to improve his product or its distribution, the client should pay.

Now Comes the Major Campaign

So, now that you've checked on product acceptance and distribution you're ready to start planning, producing, and placing your advertising. This will call into play all the different functions and activities discussed throughout this book.

MEDIA

The most brilliantly conceived and written advertisement isn't going to do anybody any good until the intended audience is exposed to it. This can be done in a great number of ways, from network television to skywriting to Web sites. The media function selects the proper vehicle or combination of vehicles to present your advertising most effectively. When properly handled this can be a truly creative function.

Let's look at the major considerations in media selection.

What to Look for in Selecting Media

The basic rule for media selection can be stated: Buy where you will reach your target audience, when and where they are most likely to buy, with the most careful and efficient utilization of the client's money. This obviously goes way beyond the old criterion of how much it costs to get a thousand readers or viewers or listeners who are located where you want them. Here are a few of the other things to look at.

The influence of the medium. Do those who see it or hear it respect it? Do they get from it important information in addition to its entertainment value? Is it essential to them or can they take it or leave it?

The appropriateness of the medium. You are looking not only for numbers of people located where they can buy your product; you seek the type of people who will buy. Are these the kind of people who are reached by this medium?

The size of the medium. Yes, costs per thousand usually go down as circulation increases, but at the same time the number of claims for the reader's attention go up. Might you do better to tell your story in a family room instead of Grand Central Station?

The success of the medium. Is it on the way up or going down? This indicates the need for up-to-date information. Try to buy what a medium is today, not what it was last year.

Duplication. Does the medium do the same job as others you are buying? Often this reinforcement is desirable, but it can be expensive.

These are only a few of the additional facts to consider. Add to them information about how long the life of the medium is, how many people see each copy, whether it's paid or free, guarantees of its circulation, any special ethnic or religious influence it may have, its influence and income demographics, and you arrive at a pretty good picture of what you are really buying.

Astute and scholarly media analysis makes the advertising dollar go far. Also, as it should, it makes a most favorable impression on the client. Here is one of several ways in which the agency can justly claim superior knowledge and prove it. There is just as much call for creative thinking in the media department as in the realm of copy and plans.

Extra Values You Can Get from Media

Any publication can give you a very detailed breakdown of the kind of audience it reaches—the demographics and maybe even psychographics of its audience—and will break down their data by postal zip codes. But you can get help from media and their representatives in a lot of other ways too.

They'll be glad to give you geographical or even climatological differences in their areas that may affect your product's sales; they'll come up with data on the advertising activities of your client's competitors; they'll make store checks and market position studies; they have available major research studies that they'll be glad to share with you.

The database has become the buzzword in the nineties. You can target your audience by marital status, income levels, age groups, by narrow geographic areas, lifestyles, buying patterns, and many other measurable statistics. The media reps are very happy to supply you with as much data as they can gather. It is in their own self-interest to do so. For example, you can buy a full-page ad in *Time* magazine and have it run only in the cities you choose.

How About Local Rates and Co-op Advertising?

Most newspapers, many radio stations, and some TV stations have local rates that are substantially lower than their national rates. The local rates are frequently not commissionable but almost always are so much lower that an agency for a client that qualifies to use local rates can add on its 17.65 percent markup and still save the client money. All noncommissionable local rate advertising placed through the agency is handled this way unless the agency is working under an overall fee arrangement calling for billing all outside purchases at net cost.

Let's look first at the handling of co-op advertising as it affects the agency for the manufacturer. You start with a definite understanding, in contract form, between the manufacturer and his outlets as regards advertising. This stipulates the amount each will pay toward the final amount expended for local advertising. Often the manufacturer will pay 50 percent of the cost of locally placed advertising, but it can run up to 75 percent or, in some cases, even 100 percent. The agency must be involved in the negotiations drawing up this agreement.

Generally the manufacturer and his agency determine the advertising approach and wording. It is not usually feasible to let local outlets change the material, since for cumulative effect all the advertising should tell the same story in the same way. Usually, therefore, this co-op advertising goes out in the form of film or veloxes for newspapers and videotapes or films for broadcast media. The dealer's name is then added locally—it's called a tag.

The dealer or other local outlet places the advertising at the local rate and pays for it in the normal course of business. Each month, then, the dealer sends tear sheets or affidavits of performance with copies of the bills to the manufacturer's agency. This agency reimburses the dealer at the agreed-upon ratio and, in turn, bills its client for his or her share. The agency, of course, adds on the standard markup.

More and more large local outlets, such as department stores and distributors, are now employing their own agencies; this can complicate the co-op picture. When such a store participates in a co-op program it naturally has its agency place the advertising and also handle the production details needed to get the store's name added to the material from the manufacturer's agency, or even to produce the whole advertisement locally.

The local agency bills its client for its services including standard markup or commission and attaches all the necessary supporting papers. The store pays its agency and passes on to the manufacturer's agency its claim for reimbursement in accordance with the co-op contract. This is where it gets sticky because, certainly, the manufacturer's agency is entitled to compensation for creating the advertising that was used locally and yet one commission has already been paid to the local agency on the space or time.

There are probably as many ways to approach this problem as there are cooperative advertising plans. One might be for the client to share with his agency the savings the client realizes as a result of using local rates. Another would be for the agency to be paid a straight fee for creating the co-op advertising, without relating this directly to the space or time used to carry the message.

My purpose here is not to draw up a catalog of methods for paying the agency, but simply to point out the problem. Agency principals becoming involved in a co-op program should take good care to investigate fully this aspect of the agreement to ensure that they will be properly compensated for their efforts.

Barter

Many years ago it was common for advertisers, such as hotels, to pay for space or time by giving due bills that could be exchanged for room accommodations. In radio and TV the practice traditionally was involved with payment for distress time—and there's nothing so worthless as time that has gone by unsold.

An article in *Advertising Age* pointed out that the practice is spreading to cover payment for time bought in the regular manner on the basis of gross rating points or other standard criteria. The difference is that the time is paid for by merchandise—even including automobiles—or a combination of merchandise and cash. This can get technical, and most barter deals are arranged through specialized agencies in New York or Chicago.

You may never come face to face with barter media buying, but you should know that it exists and can be a very important part of the buying process for some clients. When negotiating such deals, you should be aware of the tax ramifications for the client and your agency.

Now, let's cover production and trafficking the job through the agency.

PRODUCTION OF ADVERTISING MATERIAL

Of all the dramatic changes that have occurred in advertising, the production of collateral and ad material has been the most spectacular. Just a short time ago, the artist would sit at the drawing board, prepare a rough layout—drawn by hand—then order type from a typesetting house, then do a keyline (which is a paste-up of all the elements), then send it out for engravings. Yes, the changes have been spectacular!

Digital publishing technology involves the electronic capture, composure, and output of an image. This has led to the elimination of outside production facilities when preparing material for client presentations. An agency color scanner that captures images at resolutions of up to 8,000 dots per square inch provides the production staff with the ability to put together designs totally in-house. Add to these improvements the fact that the agency's software applications allow it to alter the color and structure of digital images to suit client requests.

Thus, the agency can perform its own rework projects in-house instead of returning designs to film prep houses with each additional change. This gives agencies the fast turn-around time and the quality control that was never before possible. The mechanical elements that go into the preparation of an ad start with a computer-generated layout. Then, to get to the complete ad, there is a myriad of elements such as laser proofs, color proofs, film positives or negatives (right from the in-house printer) and which in the production phase can include scans, placing images, photo manipulation, film preparation, film output, and match prints.

It is estimated that 90 percent of all small and mid-size agencies now prepare their ads and collateral materials with the computer.

RESEARCH

Do agencies need research? They can't succeed without it. No matter what you call it, it makes all the difference between seeing where you're going and flying blind. Don't fall into the common error of thinking research is only for the big shops, that smaller ones can't afford it.

Actually, the first move for an advertising person in tackling a selling problem for a client is research. The moment you look at any product or service whose sales you hope to increase, you must begin to ask questions about it, and you are up to your ears in research before you know it. Who uses the product or service? We must know this accurately before we can do any planning involving the media we will use and the message we will prepare. Where are these people? What are they like? How long have they used the product and why? What other products are there that they may use instead? What features of the product are in its favor, which are against it? What is its history? Has it been increasingly successful, or is it going downhill? Is it making or losing money? If the latter, what can be done about it? Is it a lost cause or is there hope?

These are the sort of questions that automatically should arise in the mind of any able advertising person tackling a job. There is nothing esoteric or mysterious about them. They are simply questions that should occur to any good businessperson as he or she makes plans for the promotion of any product or service. So, most research is based on just good common sense.

Often the client supplies the agency with information about the product's history, its market, and its basic character. The agency assumes the information is reliable, brushes off its own responsibility with "that's up to the client," and plunges ahead. This can be very dangerous especially in these days when agencies have been held liable for erroneous advertising and haven't been able to get off the hook by saying, "We got the information from the client."

The best policy seems to be for the agency to decide how much market and product information is needed, and then to find out how much of this information is available from the client's own organization. Unless this is done, the agency may duplicate efforts being made elsewhere.

Does this mean that an agency must have a research department? Not at all. I think the agency's responsibility is to be research-minded and sufficiently experienced to be able to ask the right questions and properly interpret the answers. You can always buy investigative work from outside sources when needed, or have your own creative people ask questions in the field. This can help them in their creative planning too. So, if a client requires it, set up a research department, but in any event keep a positive attitude toward research as one of your tools.

Who pays for research? The best general answer would seem to be the one who benefits most. If the research is to give the agency background information for choosing the proper copy appeal, or if it's intended to help select the most efficient media to carry the message, the agency should pay for it. On the other hand, if it concerns the client's product, its characteristics, its distribution, its appeal to buyers—in short, the kind of information the client should be expected to know—the client should pay. Regardless of the decision, it's vitally important that an agreement be reached about payment before any research is undertaken.

TRAFFIC CONTROL

At what point in an agency's growth does it need a special department to oversee the movement of copy and materials to meet closing dates without confusion? And, in general, how does the agency go about it?

The need for a special traffic department or individual, as is usually the case, can't be related to any set point in the growth of an agency's billings. Often a small agency will need traffic control sooner than a larger one. It depends upon the number of advertisements under preparation at any one time. An agency handling a large number of industrial accounts, for example, may need traffic control before a larger shop handling fewer national advertisements, even though they add up to more billing.

Your traffic control operation should be capable of working with broadcast, print, and Internet advertising. While the things with which it is necessary to deal are quite different for each, the basic principles on which a sound and efficient traffic control system operates are the same in all cases.

Installing and Selling Traffic Control

Management must decide, of course, when the added salary expense of a traffic specialist is justified. It's much more than a clerical job because it calls for judgment, ability to install and maintain a system, and, most of all, the executive ability to get along with people.

So, when planning traffic control, better figure on a salary in the junior executive range, plus whatever office space and equipment may be needed. It won't be a negligible expense.

The first step in implementing your traffic system is selling the system and the individual who heads it to all those in the shop with whom he or she will come in contact. No traffic control can succeed without management backing and the hearty cooperation of all agency people.

A good chief executive can easily point out to all concerned that traffic control saves time and money all along the line since it works to avoid last minute rushes, overtime work, and the inevitable errors that go along with hurried preparations for producing advertising.

What Kind of Person Do You Need?

Aside from the ability to get along with people, a successful traffic director needs to be systematic, exact, farsighted, and possessed of a considerable knowledge of all the processes that go into the preparation of advertising in all types of media. A good traffic person should know not only who does each part of a job but how it is done. He or she needs to know how long it takes to produce each element that goes into each job.

You may ask why a traffic director should have to know all these things. Isn't it enough if the production people are familiar with the technical details? No. Unless the traffic person knows exactly what he or she is asking for in the way of deliveries of art, copy, and other materials needed by a definite due date, he or she will ask for the impossible or underestimate the time required to do a job. Soon his or her credibility and authority disappears, people discount the time estimates and relapse into the previous system of getting the most urgent things out first and putting off to the last possible moment the completion of other jobs.

A prime requirement for a good traffic director is a mixture of tact and resolution. He or she has to ride herd on a temperamental bunch of account people and copy and art producers, he or she must make sure of getting his or her stuff when it's needed, and all this must be done without stepping on too many toes. Lacking authority and tact, a traffic director can create a surprising amount of resentment.

The traffic controller must know just when he or she needs whatever is asked for. Whatever date is set, he or she must stick to it, and must have the necessary experience in production to be able to explain the reason for the selected dates.

Inevitably in an agency of any size, people will be found who will do their jobs on time, accurately, and to everybody's satisfaction; and others who are always trying to catch up with themselves, about to do this or that, or busy with something else of prime importance that must be done before the required job is delivered. These people, otherwise able and valuable, must be handled with tact but also with firmness. Traffic control must control; otherwise it isn't worth the money it costs.

What Are the Best Control Techniques?

This is a question that can't be answered categorically. Some traffic managers work best with an elaborate wall chart, posted where all may examine it, showing clearly the status of each advertisement in process of preparation. It shows the dates for completion of each stage and provides for showing when each part has actually been completed. Other traffic managers find it easier to work with filing or loose-leaf systems on which the necessary control information is recorded. There are now software packages that will keep track of delivery dates and follow each job in every phase.

Whatever the mechanics of the traffic control system, there are two principles that must be followed.

The essence of traffic control on any given job is to work backwards from closing dates. Determine the normal time required for each step—art, copy, production, and the like—needed to complete the job. List these with added time between steps for internal and client OK, add them all up, and work back from the closing date to see when you have to start the job. In developing this schedule, of course, the traffic manager must work very closely with creative and production people and outside suppliers so all can accept the timetable as realistic.

Once you've worked this out, you'd do well to make up a standard timetable and distribute it to all account people so they won't make promises to the client they can't keep. Creative and production people should get copies too, so they can know what's being promised in the way of completion dates. A typical timetable for magazine ads might look like this:

Print Timetable—Single Ad*	
Preproduction	*Working Days*
Concept, Copy, and Layout	5
Estimate	2–5
Client OK	1–2
Photography/Illustration	5–10
Retouching	2
Type	2
Mechanical	1–3
Client OK	1–2
Production	
B/W (if B/W print supplied)	1–2
B/W (if 4/C transparency supplied)	5
Corrections	1
2/C	3–4
Corrections	1
4/C	5–7
Corrections	2
If client OK is needed	1–2
Shipping	1

*This table is for a "precomputer" agency. These are average days needed—the work can be produced in less time if need be, but it should not be the rule.

This is intended only to illustrate the principle because the time needed to complete different steps will vary widely from city to city and agency to agency. So check your local situation first but, once you've done so, draw up and distribute your timetable and insist that it be followed in scheduling your work flow.

The second basic principle is that the traffic manager must keep accurate and complete records on the jobs in the shop. He or she must know where each stage of each job is supposed to be and where it actually is. When can the next person due to work on it expect it so he or she can plan his or her work? Is a bottleneck developing that can be corrected by changing job assignments? Does it look as though an extension may be needed? Will overtime have to be authorized? An adequate record system administered by a knowledgeable traffic manager will anticipate these questions and plan corrective action before a crisis develops.

From all this you can see that a properly organized and operated traffic control system can result in substantial dollar savings to the agency and its clients. It also can go a long way toward enhancing the agency's reputation for operating in a businesslike manner and getting work out on time with a minimum of headaches.

For agencies not yet using the computer, here is the series of steps to put a job through your shop:

1. Account executive meets with client.

2. Account executive completes client contact form (to record information).

3. Account executive prepares job ticket/asks for quote.

4. Account executive follows up with conference report to client.

5. Account executive submits quote on cost estimate form to client for approval.

6. After approval, job is started in agency.

7. Job ticket and auxiliary time sheet is attached to job jacket.

8. Job is processed through agency for completion. (Creative department records time on time sheet.)

9. As outside invoices (and time sheets) come in for jobs, copies are filed in job jacket.

10. Job is complete, ready for billing.

11. All invoices and time sheets are recorded on job jacket.

12. Creative billing is prepared by account executive (or by bookkeeper, then approved by account executive).

13. Billing goes out regularly. For media, billing goes out before closing date; for long-term projects, bill "work in progress" every thirty days.

If you're using a computer, the same information will simply be recorded on a computer program that does automatic calculations so anyone can see immediately how much a campaign is costing.

PURCHASE CRITERIA FOR A FULL-SCALE SOFTWARE SYSTEM

In selecting a computer-based system to manage the flow of business, several criteria should be examined:

- Will the system provide support for all phases of the agency operation?
  - Accounts receivable
  - Accounts payable
  - General ledger
  - Job trafficking
  - Job estimating
  - Production billing
  - Media ordering
  - Media billing
  - Time keeping
  - Profit reporting
  - Checkbook management
- Are these modules available individually, or must they be bought as a package?
- Will it be compatible with both PC and Macintosh computers?
- Will there be adequate installation and training support?
- Is there a satisfactory continuing technical support service?
- Is there a program for providing continuing upgrades?
- Will its modules interface with the existing media department pre-buy software?
- Is the accounting module adaptable to your needs? Will it grow with you?
- Is the program easy to use and understand?
- Is the pricing favorable?
- Is financing of the payment available?

There are some systems especially for design studios and agency art departments that will track and invoice time and costs for all of your design projects; they will

- initialize and manage a docket of all your active jobs and clients
- mark up and post all your time and costs to each job, using your rates and markups
- provide reports and summaries of your jobs at any time
- invoice your jobs after automatically compiling and totaling entries using your invoice design
- automatically track open invoices and accounting activity

—18—

Public Relations—One More Element in the Successful Marketing Plan

Many professionals view public relations as unpaid advertising as compared with purely paid advertising. Generally, space in a public relations story or feature article is considered to be worth five times the value of paid advertising. Editorial copy is considered to be that much more trustworthy and believable than a paid ad. Providing a public relations capability should be an integral phase in your agency's total marketing mix.

Most agencies, particularly smaller ones, think of public relations as a vague term covering advice on responding to questions on company policy that affect popularity, implemented by nothing more than some perfunctory releases—informative material more or less well done that, it is optimistically hoped, will get published for free. Once the stuff has been sent on its way to the editorial trash basket, most agencies do nothing more to see what happened to it. But public relations is far more than that!

WHAT PUBLIC RELATIONS IS

While advertising is mostly concerned with what makes people buy, public relations goes much further into the wide range of human opinions, prejudices, likes and dislikes—motivation, if you will. It requires the best possible understanding of what makes people think and act as they do. It involves favorable contacts between the advertiser and the individuals and companies with whom it does business.

A company's public relations department looks both inward and outward. It examines the company's employees from bottom to top and endeavors to find out what will make them work most effectively. From there it spreads outward to vendors who sell to the company and to all who have anything to do with the distribution of its goods or services. Still further out, it encompasses consumers. Are they pleased, satisfied, or unhappy? Are they vulnerable to the inroads of competitors? Are they likely to stay customers of the company, or would only a small inducement swing them over into another competitor?

How about legislators whose decisions may affect the advertiser's fortunes favorably or adversely? Do they know and like the company? Are they armed in advance against unfavorable rumors or inspired releases from competitors?

How about the media that are read by individuals whose good opinion is desired? Are they in possession of all pertinent facts about the advertiser's product or service? If a possible purchaser should ask for an opinion from their editors, would it be favorable?

Public relations work, then, means shaping the policies that affect standing, credit, and reputation. It means building a backlog of favorable bias. It means adding the plus, however intangible, that gives the company possessing it a better break against competition. It should make higher prices, where they are deserved, accepted without rancor.

The Role of the Agency

I doubt that any agency can serve its client properly without being vitally interested in the advertiser's public relations. When the client has his or her own public relations department, or when an able and accredited public relations firm or individual is employed, the agency should help all it can, without criticism. But without the presence of an experienced public relations practitioner, the agency either should recommend the employment of one or become such itself.

To do this takes time and money, but often it is worth it. The agency must become familiar with many relationships far beyond those usually considered as advertising or even marketing. It must build such confidence on the client's part that even unfavorable judgments, sometimes reflecting on the client's efficiency, may be offered safely and with some chance of adoption without hurt feelings.

The timing of establishing this new and desirable relationship between client and agency is important. You don't start out by saying, "This is a new kind of arrangement, one in which we are going to do more for you, and you are going to pay us what we deserve." You must establish your value first. You must demonstrate that you have the business judgment to guide the client firm toward successful performance in its internal and external communications with all individuals and corporations in situations that affect its welfare.

In the mind of the client you become a full-scale business counselor. A good public relations adviser, in the agency or outside of it, is a prime builder and guardian of a company's reputation. No service is more important than this.

I believe that any agency, large or small, that is capable of giving its clients good business advice, which it may sell under the familiar term "public relations," will have little trouble in holding its business and being paid properly for its services.

How do you get paid for this kind of service? Invariably it is by a fee of some sort. One common method is to charge a monthly retainer that establishes the client as a regular customer entitled to seek advice from you whenever he wants. When advice is sought, you charge for whatever time your people spend on the job. Be sure you charge for every hour spent and that your rates cover your direct costs, including overhead, plus a profit.

But make sure that the individuals concerned know their business and are clearly worth what they get. Don't send a child to do an adult's work. Nowhere does ineptitude show up more quickly than in this difficult job. Nowhere can the agency damage its own standing faster. If you can't do it right, duck it completely and advise the employment of someone who can.

One delightful difference between an advertising account and a public relations account is that the latter starts generating income the minute the agency starts working with the client. If your agreement calls for starting on the 15th of February, say, your first bill to the client is for the retainer for the last half of February, usually rendered in advance.

Contrast this with an advertising account also signed up on February 15. In this case, you do your research, start writing copy, making layouts, and selecting media. Then comes production to get the message into the media. Finally, you bill the client and get your payment. This whole process can take three to four months. So it may be May or June before you receive a cent in income, and all this time you've been paying salaries and other expenses. Quite a plus for public relations.

How Publicity Is Released

For years, the procedure was to write the release, mail it out to selective publications, and call the editor and fight or beg for space. With modern, high-tech communications, there are firms that will wire, fax, and E-mail the story to several hundred media in one instant. If you are handling public relations for clients, I suggest you use one of these services to get your stories out fast and inexpensively.

—19—

Some Tips on Organizing Your Agency

When you add staff people, hire qualified, talented individuals who will help your agency grow. Amateurs will just slow you down.

With all the functions an agency performs for its clients, how do you organize for greatest efficiency? There are a lot of different ways: often a single agency uses more than one; in other instances an agency progresses from one to another as it grows; still other agencies perform some services internally and buy others from outside specialists.

Doing It Yourself

By "doing it yourself" I mean performing all, or almost all, functions internally with your own staff. It is still the basic concept on which most agencies operate, but with variations. Here are some of them.

The Jack-of-All-Trades Approach

The agency just starting out almost has to adopt this approach simply because it doesn't have a big enough staff to allow specialization. Even as an agency grows, however, it frequently makes sense to confer the responsibility for more than one function on one person.

Copy-contact is probably the most common example of this kind of organization. It finds its most frequent use on industrial accounts in which the account executive may personally write the copy. For this type of client the copy is usually highly technical. It's much more efficient if, when the client feels some change is needed, the account executive can make it on the spot instead of having to go back to the agency, explain the changes to a copywriter, and then have to fax the revised copy back to the client. This functional organization is used frequently even in large diversified agencies that may set up a separate department to handle industrial clients on this basis.

Media is often added to the responsibilities of the account executive. Again this is usually done in the case of industrial accounts in which the proper selection of media depends more on knowledge of the impact different publications will have on technical-minded groups than it does on highly sophisticated media analysis techniques.

Groups or Departments?

This question usually arises in connection with the organization of the creative function. The followers of the group concept set up creative groups, each of which may consist of one or more writers and one or more artists. They always work as a group and thus bring a total creative approach to the client's problems. Such a group may work with a single account executive and thus constitute almost a separate small agency within the whole agency. If significant broadcast advertising is involved, the group may be expanded to include an expert in broadcast production.

At the other extreme is strict departmental organization where a job is turned over to the art department or the copy department and assigned to any one of a number of people. The department head will probably try to assign the same client's work to the same person at all times, but the basic philosophy is that all staff members are generalists who should be able to work on any kind of problem.

Which type of organization an agency adopts will depend on how technical its clients' problems are and on the personalities of its staff—whether they are team players or individualists.

Modules

The ultimate expression of departmental organization is the agency that operates on the modular principle. In this case the different functions are organized as separate profit centers with almost complete autonomy. An agency offers clients the use of as many of these modular services as it wishes with no utilization of, or charge for, functions not needed. An à la carte menu, if you will.

In addition, the modular agency can offer one or more specific services to advertisers who are not regular clients. Many agencies operate in this manner. Among the services offered by agencies I know are media buying, media analysis, broadcast production, photographic studio services, public relations, and yellow page and other directory advertising. If one looked hard enough, it's quite likely that every agency service except client contact could be bought à la carte from some agency somewhere.

BUYING IT OUTSIDE

Some of the agency services I've been talking about have always been available from outside sources. Public relations is a good example; art studios are another. Many agencies, especially the smaller ones, will get rough concepts from the outside.

There are also quite a few "boutiques" that specialize in the written part of the creative package. These sell their talents on a project basis for a fee based on the time used or on a retainer basis. This plan gives the agency a call on their services up to a specified maximum in a given period of time. Some of these establishments also offer art services so they can perform the whole creative function if desired.

Another group of shops specializes in broadcast advertising. Most of these are purely production houses and thus perform services that most agencies would never perform internally in any event. Some of them, however, also include the writing function and hence properly fall in the boutique category.

Another service that can be purchased from outside sources is research. Like broadcast specialists, research firms are normally considered outside suppliers, but in some cases they, too, can take on attributes of a boutique to supplement the agency's own department.

Probably the most notable increase in the number of these outside services has been in the media field. Most of these companies started out as buying services and many still limit themselves to that function. Others have expanded to the point where they can serve as a complete media department. This service runs the whole gamut from developing objectives and strategy, through buying space or time, to approving the media invoices and paying the media. The newest service is setting up, and sometimes maintaining and updating, a Web site.

SOME OF EACH

Some agencies are organized to perform all the normal services internally, but even these agencies will use the boutiques from time to time. Maybe they have an unexpectedly heavy work load and need some help; maybe they want outside thinking as a sort of brainstorming session to inspire their own people.

Other agencies prefer not to increase their staff to perform all the agency functions themselves. They feel it's more efficient to provide broad supervision for the media buying function, for example, but have an outside service handle all the details.

Still others mix things up even more and use outside services for some clients but not for others. So the existence of these boutiques gives the agency flexibility in meeting the needs of clients. The smart agency principal is constantly aware of sources of help and what sort of help he or she can expect. It may not be needed often, but it can be a lifesaver.

Buying freelance services helps the agency keep payroll down. When you hire freelancers you pay only for work performed for clients—and your outside costs are covered.

—20—

Check Out the Value of
Agency Networks

Agency networks have proven to be very helpful and productive for independent agencies. The primary purpose of the network is to serve as a single source to help individual agencies with their day-to-day problems of running an agency, from financial guidelines, to cost controls, to new business presentations, to the managing of the staff.

What kind of agencies join networks? Well, almost any kind. Some specialize in a certain kind of client or industry, while others have very broad interests. In size they range from billings of approximately $1.2 million to $250 million and even higher, according to their listings in the *Standard Register of Advertising Agencies.*

How do networks operate? Following the principles laid down by Lynn W. Ellis, originator of the network concept, each of them is a voluntary affiliation of independent advertising agencies closely cooperating, chiefly by resident principals, to provide nationwide or even international service in line with the trend toward intensive localization of marketing campaigns. Originally, all of them operated internally through the voluntary efforts of their members, but the trend is now to a more professional approach that finds most of them with permanent, full-time paid managers.

How much do networks cost? Annual dues are usually based on the size of the agency member and can run from a low of about $500 to a high of $10,000. In addition, there are the expenses of attending meetings (usually two or three) held each year.

How can you benefit from network membership? Chiefly from access to a truly limitless source of information and help for you and your clients based on intimate local knowledge. A cardinal principle on which all networks operate is that there is not more than one member in any market, hence members don't compete with each other. So the interchange of information is free and uninhibited; questions on even the most sensitive subjects are asked—and answered—with no holds barred. In answer to questions like, "You have a savings and loan account; what appeals have you found most effective in attracting new accounts from young married people? What media mix is most effective in reaching them?" you'll get not only tear sheets, storyboards, media schedules, and costs, but an evaluation of the results obtained. Try that one on Madison Avenue.

Information also is exchanged on all manner of subjects relating to agency operations. What do you bill for? What kind of markups do you use? What's your most effective new business technique? How do you compensate your account executives? And so on.

Probably the ultimate in useful advice from one network member to another is that which results in the acquisition of a new account. Network headquarters files are full of examples of this kind of thing. Here's a specific documented example with only the names changed.

Mary, the president of an agency located in one of the Mountain states, heard that a manufacturer of outdoor sports clothing and equipment was about to select an agency. The manufacturer was well-known locally and apparently was prepared to spend enough money to give the agency a gross income in excess of $75 thousand. Very tempting, but Mary really didn't know zip about this particular industry. So what did she do?

From information available from her network, Mary learned that Dick, another network member located on the West Coast, had a lot of experience and current clients in this same industry. So, Mary got hold of Dick and was thoroughly briefed on the peculiarities of the outdoor sports business, the factors that made for success or failure, the kind of customers to seek, and how best to appeal to them.

What happened? When Mary made her presentation it immediately became apparent that she'd done her homework. She knew, and showed she knew, where the customers were, how to reach them, and how to speak the language of the trade. This head start made such an impression on the prospect that Mary got the account.

Of course, this kind of thing doesn't happen every day but, if you're successful in pulling it off only once, your network dues have paid for themselves for many years to come.

Networks have been especially helpful in the area of new business. Based on our own experience in being a member of Worldwide Partners, we have witnessed and have been part of these typical actions.

- We were making a presentation to a national chain of health food stores. We contacted five member agencies and requested that 35mm slides be made of inside displays in the various outlets located in the agencies' cities. Our presentation started out with this question: "Would you like to know how your stores look to your customers?" We were off and running and were awarded the account.

- A member agency made a request for us to visit the local pancake restaurant and make a tape recording of a member of our staff talking to their manager in front of the restaurant. The purpose was, of course, to show management that this agency had the capability to call member agencies anywhere in the country to check out their restaurants.

Another case where member agencies can help each other is when an agency is making a pitch to a major client and requests recommendation letters—informing the client that each agency will provide backup support.

As for service to you and your clients based on intimate local knowledge of the market, a recent example will make clear what can be done. An East Coast network member writes his client, "Yesterday, one of the ads we received from you was for placement in Dallas this weekend. In checking our data file, we found that Dallas has two Sunday papers . . . their circulations are equal (within 800 copies, believe it or not) . . . and their rates are exactly the same. We were told to pick the best one, which, on paper, seemed like the flip of a coin. We called our Dallas network affiliate asking their recommendation. Turns out that the *Dallas News* is vastly superior for classified help wanted—a fact only a local would know. No extra charge!"

A complaint frequently heard is that the job of an agency president is one of the loneliest in the world because you don't have anyone with whom to discuss your problems. Not so for members of networks. At regular meetings there are innumerable opportunities to talk face to face with your peers about your common problems and with members from fifteen or twenty states covering the width and breadth of the country; the wealth of information and diversity of viewpoints available is tremendous.

With members from large metropolitan areas, important regional centers, and small towns you get the benefit of the thinking of all kinds of agency people, not just the denizens of Madison and Michigan Avenues. What's more, these people are intimately involved in the day-to-day operations of their agencies and know firsthand the virtues of living within one's income and putting aside a bit for a rainy day.

With almost no large national accounts in which domination by size, color, or frequency of insertion seems to be the name of the game, network principals are up to their ears in industrial advertising, in local television shows, in couponed advertising, in direct mail—those areas of advertising in which the expenditure has to bring home the bacon, or else. As a result, they have a keen understanding of their value to clients and are not afraid to charge accordingly.

In recent years there have been a few instances of a network handling a national account—usually structured by having one member act as the flagship agency responsible for basic planning and the creative concept with outlying member agencies providing local knowledge of media, merchandising, and the like, and doing most of the local and regional contact and promotion. The number of individual members involved with any such client depends on their location in relation to the client's distribution patterns.

Once networks are mentioned, a frequent question is, "I'm a member of AAAA, so why do I need a network?" Actually, the two organizations complement, rather than compete with, each other. The personalized, noncompetitive help available to network members has already been described. AAAA can't foster this kind of interchange of sensitive information because, with many members in the same city, its members are bound to be in competition with each other and hence understandably reluctant to speak out freely.

On the other hand, AAAA is the national representative for the industry and its members handle about 90 percent of all advertising placed through agencies. Hence it can supply industry-wide statistics; maintain a comprehensive library on advertising subjects; keep its members advised about governmental and other regulations and taxes affecting advertising; and make available all kinds of group insurance plans that small networks cannot equal.

Here is the latest reported listing of independent agency networks:

Advertising & Marketing International Network (AMIN)
Glenn Jamboretz, President
One City Centre
St. Louis, MO 63101
Tel: 314-436-5455
Fax: 314-436-0365

Intermarket Association of Advertising Agencies
Walter Ohlmann, President
1605 N. Main Street
Dayton, OH 45405
Tel: 513-278-0681
Fax: 513-277-1723

Independent Agency Network
c/o William M. Claggett
1515 S. Flagler Drive, Suite 2603
West Palm Beach, FL 33401
Tel: 407-655-6973
Fax: 407-655-7169

MCAN (Marketing Communications Agency Network)
Ronald E. Launs, Inc.
c/o Lisha Fisher
24725 W. Twelve Mile Road, Suite 320
Southfield, MI 48037
Tel: 810-352-0400
Fax: 810-352-0406

Millenium Communications Group
c/o Bernie Mogelever, Managing Member
1 Dag Hammarskjold Plaza
New York, NY 10017
Tel: 212-702-4898
Fax: 212-684-6276

Mutual Advertising Agency Network
Donald A. Campbell, Executive Director
25700 Science Park Drive
Cleveland, OH 44122
Tel: 216-292-6609
Fax: 216-292-6780

North American Advertising Agency Network
Robert Purcell, President
245 Fifth Avenue
New York, NY 10016
Tel: 212-481-3022
Fax: 212-481-3071

Second Wind Advertising Services
Tony Mikes
1120 Hobart Avenue
Suite C
Wyomissing, PA 19610
Tel: 610-374-9093
Fax: 610-374-9238

Transworld Advertising Agency Network (TAAN)
Jack Warner, Chairman
Warner, Bicking, Morris & Partners
866 UN Plaza, Room 407
New York, NY 10017
Tel: 212-759-7900
Fax: 212-759-8087

Trans-Canada Advertising Agency Network
Bill Whitehead, Executive Director
3390 Bayview Avenue
North York, Ontario
Canada M2M 3S3
Tel: 416-221-8883
Fax: 416-221-8260

Worldwide Partners
Patricia J. Fiske, President
2280 S. Xanadu Way, Suite 300
Aurora, CO 80014
Tel: 303-671-8551
Fax: 303-337-9576

— Part V —

New Business— The Lifeblood of an Agency

—21—

Locating Your Prospects

An old maxim of the advertising agency business goes like this: *Every day you come to work you are one day nearer to the time when you are going to lose your largest account.* This statement may seem like negativism, but it drives home the point that an agency can at any time lose a major source of income, often for reasons beyond its control.

Another precept can be added to this: *Client budget allocations may suddenly be reduced, but not client demands for the same level of service.*

So, there is the double bind that agency operators face: the uncertainties of income flow and the need to maintain service to protect the budgets that remain.

Most advertising agencies want to keep their staff members together and productive. They can't do that unless management recognizes and fulfills their individual hopes for the future. This requires a dynamic and growing agency, which means new business must be developed.

These two overriding considerations—survival and the need to grow—dictate that an agency's top management must consider new business one of its primary responsibilities and must organize to seek it.

New business seldom just falls in your lap. *You have to work for it—continuously!*

As good as your agency may be, prospects have to be constantly and convincingly told about what you have to offer and how they can benefit from it. It's fine to build a better mousetrap, but don't believe that old story about the world beating a path to your door. Put the trap on display and have a mouse in it.

WHO ARE YOUR PROSPECTS AND WHERE ARE THEY?

No doubt about it, your best new business prospects are your present clients. You know them and they know you. Presumably you're doing a good job for them or you'd have been replaced already. If you're doing a good job for them, their sales will grow and, as a result, their advertising expenditures will probably expand. They may be opening up new territories. They may be bringing out new products or buying companies in related lines of business. Because you know these people you've got the inside track.

When you look beyond your present clients, start with a market survey. The need for this is as evident in new business development as it is when doing a selling job for your clients. The product you seek to sell is your agency. Who will buy it, where are they, in what lines of business, and how large are they? These questions concerning the market for your own services must be answered in a professional way.

In general, an agency is best at soliciting accounts in lines of business they know something about, or for which they have an affinity. An agency wastes its time if it pitches for accounts that are too large for it to handle or which require specialized knowledge that the agency doesn't possess. Some would say that an agency shouldn't solicit accounts that are located too far away, but this is a rule that is being countered by the immediacy of action allowed by E-mail, fax, computer file downloading, and video conferencing.

It's fine to be optimistic, but the basic idea is that it is better to be realistic. An agency's resources to chase new business are not unlimited, so it is better to concentrate on a few accounts of highest potential. This permits that effort to be more intensive and that increases the chance of a successful result.

INDUSTRY

First, concentrate on industries in which you have experience, either directly or in closely related fields. If you've handled bank advertising it's not too far a cry to go after other financial businesses such as securities brokers, mortgage companies, personal loan firms, etc. If you handle an industrial pump company, handling an electric motor company would not be too different. But this experience would mean little to a manufacturer of package goods sold to homemakers.

When doing an inventory of your agency experience, don't over-look the experience some of your people may have had before they came to you. Get each of them to list all industries they've been involved with and you may be surprised at the number of industries covered. Americans are a highly mobile people both geographically and job-wise and unexpected talents turn up all over the place.

GEOGRAPHY

Modern travel is fast—you know, breakfast in London, lunch in New York, dinner in San Francisco (don't try doing it in reverse)—but also expensive. So keep both time and expense of travel in mind when thinking about soliciting out-of-town prospects.

In setting geographic limits think about whether you can get to an out-of-town client's city, do business, and return in the same day. Be sure to factor in airline late arrival time probability, rush hour taxi time from the airport to the client, then back to the airport. Just as a gauge of what is feasible, there are many South Florida clients using New York agencies and vice versa. Then there are New York agen-cies that handle accounts in Los Angeles, but these are mostly accounts with large budgets that justify layover expense or even a local service office or company apartment.

However, distance can be turned into a positive factor. For exam-ple, a western state agency was handling a local bank that became a bank holding company and began acquiring local banks all over its state. The agency had to visit each of these outlying banks at regular intervals, which began to take a lot of time and money. So the agency made a virtue out of necessity. It started actively soliciting new clients in the cities where the local banks were. As a result, it obtained more clients and was able to service several on each trip.

Another San Francisco agency refined the principle by doing the same thing, but narrowed its coverage problems by only soliciting clients in the same industrial park as one of its existing clients. One call then could cover multiple clients.

SIZE

Size works two ways. First, don't bite off more than you can chew. Big accounts can be fine but not if they are so large in relation to the size of the agency that they can't be handled without seriously reducing the amount and quality of service to other clients. Well, you may say, why not staff up to handle the account? This makes sense up to a point, but you can't service an important account with all new people. In fact, an agency usually has to promise the service of key staff members in order to bring in a large new account. So, the agency is faced with the need to maintain a nucleus of people who can provide the necessary direction and input that will carry on the agency's standards of quality and service.

At the other extreme are the very small accounts. These can chew up a lot of staff time while producing very little income. It's tempting to take on accounts like these because they can generate incremental income with no addition to staff. The trap here is that, if staff people servicing existing accounts must handle this additional business, they may have to reduce the quality and amount of service given to the existing accounts.

If the small account has real potential to develop, by all means take it on as an investment in the future. But watch it carefully and don't hang onto it if it becomes apparent that the account isn't going to grow. The kinds of accounts that can have the greatest future potential for an agency are special projects or divisions of very large accounts. Do good work and the odds are high that you will get more business from other parts of the client company.

WHO SHOULD WORK ON
NEW BUSINESS?

Two agencies I know answer this question simply, if not simplistically. One, in Missouri, tells its people "New business is your business"; the other, in Wisconsin, says "New business is everybody's business." No doubt both of these statements point up the vital role new business activity plays in an agency's scheme of things, but they hardly represent a sound blueprint for organizing the new business function.

The ideal new business setup within the agency is a separate department headed by an individual skilled in agency selling. This, however, is completely impractical except for the largest shops. Small agencies cannot afford the salary burden of individuals who perform only the soliciting function. The results are almost invariably too uncertain and too far off in time.

In small agencies, new business responsibility must be assumed by the principals. Theoretically, they should allocate a substantial part of their time (some say as much as a third) to seeking new billing to replace that which is normally lost, to provide growth, and to ensure the future of their business. But you know how it is: clients and service first, new business when you have time or when you're clearly in trouble.

So for the smaller shops, the solution would be to name a seasoned executive of management stature to head a new business committee as a permanent assignment. This need not be a full-time job, but the executive, with the help of a capable assistant, should build a file of suitable prospects of a size, character, and location the agency could profitably serve.

The new-business person should assign suitable people to contact each of the names on this list, preferably about once a month. Then he or she should make sure the results of each contact are carefully noted so the record will always be complete.

As you can see, this way of going after new business is far from automatic. It requires personnel be constantly and consistently used with intelligence and adaptability. Delegate certain suitable persons to spend part time on this work, but see that the time is allocated and used because agencies now know that getting new business is not simply desirable, it is essential. Either you grow or you are on the way out in this business.

Definite time allocated and personal contacts with prospects—that's the formula, and the only one that works.

—22—

Getting Down to New Business

There are many new business plans that an agency can follow to get new business. Here are some techniques that have worked for small agencies; any one of these plans may better fit your agency's personality and structure:

- The Active Approach
  - Have one of your staff make constant calls to set up appointments for principals. Put someone in charge to handle the new business program.
  - Hire an outside new business specialist to handle the entire program, from handling mailings to cold calls. (This generally has not worked for small agencies.)
  - Contact all media representatives—have a breakfast, thank them for their help, and ask for leads or recommendations.
- Direct Mail
  - Business-to-business mailings
  - Third-dimensional mailings
  - Personal direct mail letters
  - Newsletters

- More Long-Range Approaches
  - Making contact in various civic and charitable organizations
- Publicity/feature articles
- Ask for referrals from clients and friends

There are, of course, many variations of each of these programs. Following is a condensation of *Business Development Audit for Agencies*, published by The Lustig Company of North Miami, Florida, and printed here with permission. This program will give you dozens of ideas on how to get new business.

Agency Promotional Activities

Why is it that the shoemaker's children so often have no shoes? Agencies that can go on infinitely in generating public relations and promotional activities for clients, often do nothing for themselves. Could it be that advertising/public relations agencies do not think of themselves as being promotable? If so, consider the following areas of potential activity:

Open House at the Agency

Agencies spend a lot on rent in elegant buildings and on decor and furnishings. The rationale is usually that "We need to look like a successful agency when clients and prospects come in." But how often do prospects come in? The answer is, of course, not very often. That is because most agencies do nothing to bring them in.

So, let's look at some ways to entice prospects to come see the offices of which you are so proud. First, there is the opportunity that arises when you move to new quarters or redecorate old quarters. Hold an open house that features some sort of interesting focal point.

- Have an art show for a talented local artist.
- Bring in a celebrity from local television.
- Bring in a sports star from a local team.
- Ask the mayor or governor to come by and feature his or her presence.
- Put together a multimedia show that features your agency's work.

- Have a noted local chef do things in your new model kitchen.
- Have an artist do caricatures of the invitees.

Stepping back a level from such structured events, offer the use of your agency's conference room and audiovisual facilities for meetings of certain community groups. Look for groups that have top management people on their committees. Even if you do not get specific new business prospects into your shop this way, you can count on the fact that there will be comments passed around the community about your shop—comments that might reach those you want to impress.

Advertising in Media

There are few agencies that haven't tried advertising services in magazines or newspapers. The common complaint is that nothing happened. The reason is that there is rarely a specific proposition presented that calls for immediate action. To get this type of advertising to produce, it is not enough to say you are good and you are here.

If you want to see something happen, provide the response devices to bring action—a tear-out return card asking the prospect to call for an appointment, a coupon requesting literature, an 800 telephone number . . . those devices you *know* you should use but get talked out of by the art directors.

Creation/Syndication of Broadcast Programs

This avenue of action serves to publicly identify your firm as being an authority in certain fields. This is the path that has been taken by some investment people and real estate salespeople. The strategy here is to create a radio or television program piece that can be run on a continuing basis. Such pieces might be based upon such subject matter as:

- news of happenings in the local advertising/public relations industry
- news of happenings in specific local business categories
- a salute to local citizens or corporations for community support

Continuous Mailings to Prospects

Almost every agency has done mailings of some sort to prospects. Most typically it is a brochure that talks about the agency's clients, shows some of its work, and profiles its key people. This type of piece has two failings:

- It is inwardly directed. It talks about the agency, not about matters that may be more critical to the prospect.

- It is a one-shot. At the time the piece is mailed to prospects, they may not be in a frame of mind to consider an agency change. So, the piece, if it is kept, will be put in a file where it languishes until the secretary cleans out the files. Perhaps the prospect will be thinking about agency review later in the year, but the agency that did the one-shot mailing will likely not be at the top of his or her mind.

The most effective mailing vehicle to get new business prospects to raise their hands is a mailing that goes out at monthly intervals and that addresses issues that are pertinent to the prospect's area of business. Such a mailing can be either a newsletter or a series of thinkpieces. We favor the thinkpieces because the newsletter format has become overused. Newsletters have an aura of one-size-fits-all syndication. In other words, they can be viewed as a piece of canned material the agency has bought from an outside source. The thinkpiece is a two-page document discussing vital marketing communications matters that are specific to the prospects' category of business. This means that prospect lists must be developed for specific business categories such as medical/health care, retailing, business-to-business, etc. Then the pieces must be written to talk about subjects in terms of each specific industry.

It is valid to develop subjects that are fundamentally generic, i.e., suitable for any industry, but the language must be adjusted to fit the industry addressed. Typical of generic subjects would be a piece on effective direct mail practice or a discussion of how agency and client can live together more harmoniously. Such pieces should be interspersed with pieces that deal with matters indigenous to the industry.

Set these pieces up with an attractive masthead, but keep the body of the pieces looking like a Kiplinger Report or a University of California Diet Letter. Emulate pieces for which subscribers pay good money to get useful information.

More on Newsletters/Thinkpieces

We have found newsletters or thinkpieces to be the single most effective thing an agency can do to get a new business prospect to raise his hand. In our discussions with advertising agencies from coast to coast, we have repeatedly heard principals say that they have "thought about" doing this or are "going to" do it. Yet, only a minuscule percentage have followed through on getting out such letters on a consistent basis throughout the year.

The problems of getting into this kind of publishing are manifold. First of all, somebody in the agency must be found who has the capability of doing the job right—and who will have the discipline to get the pieces out each month. Then there is the problem of running the gauntlet of internal review. Everyone in the shop has different ideas about what should be said and how it should be said. In the end, the agency usually builds a camel.

The agencies that have succeeded at this have assigned the job to a high-ranking writer, one who is allowed to make it his project . . . without interference. However, even this person will probably need input from others in the shop in order to develop sufficient editorial material.

The alternative is to buy a newsletter or thinkpieces from an outside specialist. Because it is critical that these pieces be aimed at a target audience, it is recommended that you hire an outsider to handle this project. When you become the client, you will find that the job gets done for you.

Speaking Engagements

If you have ever been the program chairman of an organization that has weekly or monthly meetings, you are aware of the continuing problem of finding speakers. Most advertising agency principals are good on their feet.

Prospect Lists

How is an agency going to go after new business in a structured manner if the prospects have not been identified? This is basic to everything you do in the new business arena. Yet, most agencies do not have well-developed prospect lists. Here is how we have gone about developing lists:

1. Start with the prospect names you do have in your files. However, review them to be sure that they are still active prospects. Many changes take place in a year's time and your names may have been in the files for much longer than that.

2. Go to the industrial directories, such as *Thomas Register.* Select by SIC categories those in which you are interested and geographically according to the territory you can comfortably service.

3. Try to acquire or borrow industry trade association membership directories.

4. Go through newspaper special sections (travel section, real estate section) and magazines and note who the major advertisers are.

When you are through doing your archiving, compile your lists alphabetically by business category and by geographic location. You may opt to have an A list and a B list, based on the importance of the prospect to you. The A list would get the heaviest attention, of course.

Then, call in a couple of your friendly media sales reps and ask them to review your lists and tell you who the real agency-change decision maker is in each firm. They will know whether it is the advertising manager, the marketing director, the president . . . or whomever. Also ask them who should be on your list that you have missed.

Gift Mailing Items

This is an approach that should be reserved for the very-hard-to-reach individual at the prospect company. If the prospect is of extreme importance to you and if you have failed to get your communications past the executive secretary who screens calls and mail, send the person something that has an appearance of value. Secretaries will rarely take it upon themselves to deprive their boss of anything that has significant monetary value.

Along with the gift goes a low-key message to the effect that you would appreciate it if he would allow his secretary to put through your next call. Or, better yet, tell her to set up an appointment for a visit with you. Or, you can have the gift delivered by local messenger service.

Here are gift ideas we have seen work effectively to reach presidents of major companies.

- An umbrella that folds down to pocket size. The accompanying message relates to the wisdom of having some kind of an umbrella when it starts to rain. Your agency is identified as the umbrella he may reach for when it rains on his current agency relationship.

- A silver plated piggy bank. The message relates to the economic advantages of using your agency.
- A monopoly game. The tie-in thought is that your agency can help him be a winner in the world where the money is real.
- A chrome-plated police whistle. Naturally, the message is, "Just whistle and we'll be there."

The gifts can be mailed in a series, and each mailing contains a response card. The whistle is the last in the series of mailings.

Wall-Hung Agency Work Samples

Most agencies will display their work in the reception room. However, we are surprised to find that many agencies show none. Show pride in your work by displaying it. If it has won awards, hang the plaques or certificates adjacent to examples of the winning campaign.

GETTING IT DONE

The major reason behind the failure of advertising agencies to have a consistent new business development program is simply that the best laid plans just don't get executed. There is always a rationale for not getting the job done:

- So much new business has been coming in by gravity we haven't needed it.
- We are so busy with client work, we haven't been able to do it.
- We haven't had time to work on developing a prospect list.
- We have to make a decision as to what activity will best reflect the agency.
- We started a program but the new business development director left us.

The litany of excuses goes on infinitely. But most of these reasons are quite hollow. For example, the new business rush alibi ignores the fact that the agency business is very streaky. The agency that is hot this year can find itself ice cold the next year. Then, lacking an in-place business development program, they proceed to develop one. But getting it going requires time, and there may be a long new business dry spell.

"Busy with client work" is a chronic condition in agencies. But an agency can never be *too* busy to tend to its new business development.

The development of a prospect list can, with management direction, be handled by clerical people. The matter of making decisions on what best reflects agency image is secondary to doing something that will bring the agency to the forefront with prospects. *Then* you can shape your agency image when you have a chance to get face-to-face with the prospect.

So, the new business director left. Did he or she not leave the legacy of an in-place program that can be delegated to someone else? If not, the agency is not using this function correctly.

We have belabored the point here, because we have seen that the new business development function is a stepchild in most agencies. Yet, failure to have such a program is a prime reason why agencies fail. One thing is sure in the agency business: clients come and go and unless an agency keeps bringing in new business, it will inevitably decline.

With all this in mind, let's take a look at actions and disciplines for getting the job done.

Taking Personal Responsibility

Here is the bad news: there is no passing the buck down the line when it comes to primary responsibility for new business development. New business development must be driven by the CEO of the agency. There are at least two basic reasons for this. The first is that, internally, new business development activities will be downgraded in priority if it is not seen that the leader wants them kept at the top of the "to do" list. The second reason is that, in initial contacts with prospects, subordinates don't carry the weight of the president, chairman, or CEO. *Every prospect wants to feel that he or she is of such importance that he or she will get the full attention of the agency's very top management.*

We have repeatedly witnessed vows of personal involvement from the leaders of giant, multinational agencies when facing a new business prospect. Common sense tells you that these people can't possibly have enough time to serve every account on their long list. Yet prospects want to hear this. There appears to be a suspension of disbelief on the part of the prospect. As long as the leader of the agency shows up a couple of times a year at meetings with the client, once the prospect becomes a client, there is usually no problem.

But the critical issue is that during the courtship process, the agency leader should be in the forefront of client/prospect interface. This establishes a bond of confidence.

Another way for the CEO to lead new business recruitment is to leave the basic responsibility with the CEO and assign backup support to the various specialized functions. Assign a copy writer and art director to work on new business generation materials. Have an account executive back up the CEO in supervising internal functions for the new business program.

Assigning Backup New Business Responsibility

The two most common arrangements for delegating new business development activity are the appointment of a full-time new business director or the assignment of new business development to an account service person.

In the first scenario, the advantage of the full-time new business director is that this person is not diverted into other activities. One disadvantage is that, if successful, he or she will usually find that the accounts brought in will want that person to work on their account. Then the position loses its functional integrity. Another is that, if the person fails to produce, he or she will be discharged or resign. Then begins the revolving door syndrome, with new business directors coming and going.

If using the second arrangement, the advantage of having an account service person do double duty between account work and new business development is that there will be stability, even if the new business development aspect is not totally successful. The other side of the coin is that there is less incentive for this person to produce new business. He or she always has account work to rely on if little new business is generated.

Prioritizing New Business Work

New business work includes the preparation and issuance of an agency's continuing communications with prospects as well as the follow-up required to make it effective.

Getting out the materials each month should become as routine as paying the rent or writing paychecks. The production and dissemination activities should be delegated to the people who normally do these things. The creation of each month's mailing pieces will be the place where hang-ups are most likely to occur. Therefore, it is essential that times of light load on the creative department be utilized to work ahead on this material so you have a bank of pieces to draw on.

If it gets to a choice between getting out some client work or preparing a new business presentation, favor the new business activity. Client work can often be delayed, but the new business brass ring only comes around once. Consider new business presentation opportunities as perishables, like vegetables at the supermarket. When their time is past, all goes down the drain.

This latter choice may sound like heresy. The standard agency viewpoint is that the clients must always come first. The rebuttal to this is that the *agency* must come first and new business is the lifeblood of the agency. Clients can almost always be managed when there is a time crunch. If a client is lost because of delaying his work in favor of new business activity, balance this against the importance of developing a *flow* of new business opportunities. In the long run, this will be the success of the agency.

Timetabling for Continuity

There is little to say on this subject that any agency operator won't know about. The basis of timetabling is to have, in written form, a schedule of activities for new business. Agencies typically will put in work orders to get some new business material produced, but will fail to have the year's new business activities blocked out on a calendar. Once this calendar is done, it should be plugged into the traffic department.

Applying Discipline to Follow-Up

If the agency has a traffic manager, it should be his or her responsibility to see that the new business jobs get done. If they are not going to get done, the manager must report to the agency head and get a reassignment of due dates. If there is no traffic manager, due dates for new business work should be on the calendar of the agency head. In actuality, the executive secretary can set up this calendar and alert the agency leader as to what is due each day.

We have made this simplistic statement because we wish to emphasize that continuing new business activities can too easily be pushed into a corner and forgotten. We see it happen all the time.

Setting Criteria for Measurement of Performance

People become disenchanted with programs when no apparent results are noticed. It is true that the only ultimate measure of success is the business it brings in. Yet there are benefits that will accrue from a new business development program that may pay off in the long term, if not in the short. So, it is imperative that some measurement checks be established to see what is happening along the path toward acquiring business.

If, at the end of a year, you have had lunch three times with the decision maker at a targeted prospective account, but no business has been obtained, is this a failure? Considering that years can elapse before an account changes agencies, perhaps you still may have accomplished something. Maybe next year will be the time of change and you will get a call.

You'll get a feel for what is going on if you keep records that will allow for periodic reports on the following results:

- return of response cards asking that you continue mailings
- return of cards that ask you to add the name of somebody else in the prospect firm
- return of cards that ask you to contact the prospect for an appointment
- phone calls from prospects as a result of your new business contact efforts
- letters from prospects thanking you but saying they are not currently thinking of an agency change
- appointments made and kept as a result of the new business communications program
- speeches made to industry groups as a result of the new business development program
- visit to agency premises as a result of the new business communications program
- potential for acquisition of an account as judged by the person making the contact (near-term, mid-term, long-term)
- media mentions of the agency resulting from program efforts
- business gained directly from new business program

As the numbers begin to pile up in these reports, the agency head will be able to make a judgment as to whether the program has taken him or her anywhere . . . and whether it appears that results will be forthcoming.

Staying with the Winners

Young & Rubicam once ran an ad in advertising magazines with a headline that went something like this: "Slow down the parade, the elephants can't keep up with the bandwagon." Their message was that by the time the general public is beginning to absorb a concept expressed in an advertisement, the advertiser is already moving on to a new concept. The principle behind this is that those who are closest to the work become oversaturated with it and bored, so they move on before their customer audience has absorbed it.

This happens in agency-generated new business programs. There is often a compulsion to do something new before the full effect of the current work has been felt. If the agency didn't get a new account in the first six months, it may feel the program has failed. However, it should be recognized that a program that can generate a significant piece of new business within a year should be deemed a success. In fact, we have seen programs that didn't pay off until the second year— and were eminently worthwhile in terms of the billings generated.

If, by the measurements previously listed, the program is causing forward motion, the most productive course is to stay with it. However, if all measurements indicate that nothing of consequence has happened during nine to twelve months of use, it is time to try something else.

Testing Alternative Approaches

It is good practice to be developing alternative approaches to new business development while the current program is still running. This may be a matter of trying something quite different, or doing a modification of the present program to further energize it.

Assuming that an agency is doing a mailing program to four or five hundred names, which is quite common, a test may be run by breaking out every fourth name and running the new program with that list. A modification may be a special offer for those prospects who respond within a specific period of time. This offer may be a piece of free custom-designed research or an offer to do a gratis client newsletter (contingent on the agency being given some business). At a lower level, the offer may be a special report compiled by the agency on aspects of marketing in certain categories of business. The latter may be tied in to an opportunity to meet the prospect and talk with him or her.

All these paths to "Getting It Done" are at the heart of any new business program. The road to bankruptcy is paved with agencies that had good intentions—but didn't get it done.

BUSINESS DEVELOPMENT VIA THE INTERNET

What about the use of the Internet to generate new business leads? This is a subject of discussion in every agency that doesn't have an Internet site. Should we or shouldn't we have a home page?

The answer is that no agency in business today can afford *not* to have an Internet site. The basic reason is that today's clients are almost universally interested in what is happening on the Internet and they expect their advertising agency to be up to speed on the subject. An agency that doesn't have a home page on the Web runs the risk of being regarded as being behind the times. So, how can such an agency expect to pick up a new client who is Internet oriented?

What can an agency expect from an Internet site of its own? In general, the answer is that it depends on what is done with the site. The agency that simply publishes a few pages of copy from the agency brochure onto its site pages may not see much of anything happen. It is important to remember that the Internet is an interactive medium and to get a visitor to the home page to go through the pages, and to return to the site, there has to be some action there.

The old rule for getting attention to copy applies here: offer the reader something of value if you want to have your advertisement read. In the case of the Internet this means offering *information* of value at the site. Alternatively, site traffic can be increased by having some *action of a promotional nature*. Contests, audience participation activity, and value-added offers can generate increased interest and participation.

Importance of the Directories

At this juncture, it is estimated that a new site is being added to the Internet every 90 seconds. This means that there are such a multitude of sites out there it is necessary to provide directions to the location of your site. Not many people are going to find you by accident, so the key to getting action is the directories developed by the search engines. Site owners must send informational copy to the search engine services that will be used in the listings generated by the search engines. This copy, which describes your site, will vary in length from 20 to 80 words, depending on the requirements of the search service. It should contain keywords that an Internet user seeking information about advertising agencies might use—as many of these words as possible.

Do It Yourself or Hire It Done?

There is software available that will enable an agency to publish its own pages on the Web. However, unless an agency has a sophisticated understanding of the technology of Internet page management, an organization with depth of knowledge should be employed to set up and maintain the site. There can be a considerable difference in the access time to each page and in how fast the information comes up—differences that affect the length of time a visitor will stay with and return to a site. Typically, Web surfers have little patience and won't stay in a slow-reaction site.

—23—

The Formal Presentation

In surveys on the efficacy of agency presentations, it has been shown that the most important element in presenting to clients is the chemistry between the potential client and the agency people.

This chapter contains a compendium of ideas—things to look for and things to do when making a presentation—while, of course, retaining your own agency style and personality.

These thought stimulators will help you do a better job of maximizing your creative, marketing, and presentation efforts.

- You are selling enthusiasm, ability, and spirit. You are convinced that your program is absolutely the best the client could possibly hope for.

- Everything should be demonstrated from the prospect's viewpoint. How can you solve the client's problem? Not how great are you at coming up with wonderful ideas. Ask yourself the question, "If I were them, would I want these agency people working for me?"

- Always, always, always ask for the order.

- Show each element as it fits into the entire marketing plan—not as an isolated item.

- Use these openers *only* if you do them well:
  - humor . . . but related to the product, service, or theme

- a startling statistic or fact about their industry or business

    True-life experience: My agency made a presentation to a major bank that had just fired its president. The agency knew about this, and the week before the presentation it interviewed customers on the street to get their opinions of the bank. Responses were recorded. The feedback was not very complimentary. I started out my presentation with "Would you like to know what your customers think about your bank?" This got the prospect's immediate attention—and the agency sailed on from there.

- Have one person in charge so the meeting is kept right on schedule.

- Always have an agenda. When the conversation wanders you can use it to bring them back on track.

- Be very specific in repeating what the assignment is. Get an approval . . . ask questions that will get them to nod their heads in agreement. Get them used to saying "yes" to you.

- Another idea for the opening: ask a pertinent question regarding the program. Get them to talk and discuss it. This conversation could give you guidance for your subsequent remarks. It also gives you an opportunity to evaluate each person's style, attitude, and concerns.

- Establish a position that you are already working for the client: "Your media schedule includes . . . "

PRESENTATION TECHNIQUES

- Always concentrate on eye contact . . . but not just with the key decision maker.

- Make sure that *everyone* (on both sides) has something to say.

Ron Huff, who has served as a creative director and executive VP of large agencies, has made literally hundreds of multimillion-dollar presentations. He has authored a book on presentations called *I Can See You Naked—A Fearless Guide to Making Great Presentations.* He makes these comments: "The first ninety seconds of any presentation are crucial. Their eyes are taking snapshots of you, impressions are being registered. It doesn't take long for their minds to react. Presentation is a skill where preparation and attitude are apparent almost instantly."

How do you start off the crucial first ninety seconds?

You start by focusing on someone on the client's side; one who is committed to your support. Once you've established contact, lock in. Let eye contact register. Let the person know by your manner that he or she is very important.

Once you've made a friend in the audience, you can move on to another face, lock in, and read the reaction. This is called *warming up* the audience.

Say something that is easy for you to say (that is relevant). Maybe it's one line, a favorite quote, a relevant question, a startling or controversial statement, or a statistic from the client's industry. This gets immediate attention.

SUCCESSFUL TRICKS OF THE TRADE

1. When presenting an idea, take some obvious/easy-to-arrive-at ideas (the type of ideas that other agencies are likely to have presented). Demonstrate how bad they are and then present your own better idea.

2. Buy radio and television spots. Have receiving sets in the conference room and time things so you can play them live, off the air, during your presentation.

3. After the pitch and just before decision time, send a tape recorder over to the client's office with a cassette with your special message asking for the order.

4. Present focus group reactions to client's previous commercials.

5. Buy stock: Purchase one share of stock, then identify yourself as a shareholder. State that this gives you incentive to make the company succeed.

6. Have a current client at the presentation. Current client stays behind and answers questions about your shop.

7. Show testimonials from other clients on slides or videotape. They tell how great your agency is and enthusiastically recommend your agency.

8. Show the activities of your staff in civic organizations. Emphasize that your people are involved with the community.

9. Do research on the prospective client's distributors, dealers, and customers. Clients always want to know what people think about their products or services.

10. Leave a client with a homing pigeon—leave a pigeon in a cage. Ask client to put a message on its leg and send the pigeon back with the verdict.

11. Make it entertaining/imaginative/enjoyable.

12. Review the agenda at the start of the meeting. Confirm the amount of time to be taken . . . and don't go over your time limit unless invited *by the client.*

13. No canned speeches. Allow for interruptions and questions.

14. When talking to marketing directors, they want to hear presentations in terms of sales, leads, competition, and share of market. When talking to creative people, discuss ideas.

15. Show accountability. We're good business partners. We'll handle your money carefully . . . will, in effect, *invest* it wisely for a good return *to you.*

16. Don't discuss compensation specifics during the presentation.

17. Show the next steps. Show due dates. This demonstrates discipline, confidence, a sense of order, and professionalism.

18. Flip charts are a good way to focus interest.

19. Show case histories. These are powerful. Show how your thinking and problem solving can solve their business problems.

20. Format for case histories:
    - First, present the results.
    - State the situation in a worst-case scenario.
    - Present your idea/strategy.
    - Talk about tactics used to achieve the results.

21. In discussing agency size, don't emphasize the number of people. Talk about capabilities, i.e., media/direct response expertise, a core of specialists.

22. Always have specific questions ready to ask—to keep the momentum going.

23. Always involve the audience.

24. If you don't get the account:
    - Always conduct a postmortem. Why did you lose?

- Ask questions of the client.
- Keep after the client. Six months later can be a reconsideration point.

THE PRESENTATION FORMAT

Much has been written and critiqued about how to present your program to the client. There are as many ways to do this as there are situations. Again, let's stick to the basics.

Each presentation must include (and not necessarily in this order):

- Definition of the objective of the presentation so you will get agreement. Find out what is on their minds.
- Client talk opportunity: You must listen to the clients. Let them talk so you can gather information and evaluate the mindsets of the players.
- Show the client what's in it for him to hire your agency.
- Project enthusiasm and professionalism.
- Demonstrate problem-solving capabilities.
- Demonstrate knowledge and experience vis-à-vis your client's business and industry by doing research and playing it back.
- Show credentials and samples of creative work, but keep it as brief as possible.
- Present what ideas you have in a fresh and dramatic way.
- Show your agency as a business partner.

THE "LEAVE-BEHIND" PIECE

Always, *always* distribute the leave-behind piece *after* the presentation is made. This document should include:

- Agency credentials: your people, your clients, your results, your difference.
- Research: what was done for the client's company.
- Analysis of the market: your marketing plan and strategy.
- A detailed media plan: should include your negotiation skills and your expertise in media strategy.

- Creative approach: includes layouts, comps, videos. Just cover the broad strokes.
- References: financial, clients, creative, and media.
- How the account will be handled: which principals will be involved. Name account service and creative team.
- Compensation arrangements: spell them out in this document.
- Letter of agreement: This is your contract.

LITTLE THINGS THAT COULD MAKE A BIG DIFFERENCE

- Supply note pads and pencils with your company logo.
- Have a preset seating arrangement. Don't make the conference table a battlefield. Alternate seating positions between agency and client people.
- Put client products on display on your premises.
- Have client introduce his people first.
- Make sure every prospect in the room gets to say something.
- Match the client's dress style, if you know what it is. Dress is important.
- After the presentation, escort client to doorway or elevator.
- Do not pass out the "leave-behind" program description ahead of time.
- Use visuals. The more you use them to reinforce your key points, the easier your presentation will be to understand and remember.

THE FROSTING ON THE CAKE

When the presentation is over, your work hasn't ended. Until the decision is made, send constant reminders to the client about what you had said and shown. Remind them of any special offers you made to them and any deadlines on those offers.

Then, when you get the account, invite the new client to an agency victory party!

WHEN'S THE BEST TIME TO PRESENT?

It is physically impossible for a client to judge agency desirability properly when several meetings a day are scheduled with a dozen or more agencies that have seemed eligible to serve him. No more than one meeting a day should be planned, and no more than three in any one week. Both parties need that much time to prepare for the meetings and to digest whatever is produced in the presentations.

It is bad judgment, and bad psychology, to try to speed up the process; hurried, high-tension meetings create serious pressures. It is in the agency's best interests to resist becoming a part of any such procedure. Here, right at the beginning of the contacts between agency and prospect, the agency should make clear the need for a normal atmosphere in which to present its case. Of course, this is easier said than done. Usually the agency takes whatever situation is offered and does the best it can. But it is highly desirable, in prepresentation contacts, when the coming conference is informally discussed, that the agency make this important point.

A prospect is favorably impressed by an agency attitude that emphasizes the importance of the meeting and resists being pushed into haste or time limit restraints. All these considerations come into the psychology of the presentation. The relationship being considered by both parties needs to be entered into with care and deliberation. Only then has it a chance to become permanent and confer all the benefits it should upon both agency and client.

If a whole series of presentations is being made, as is usually the case, the agency would be wise to try to appear either first or last. The first agency to present can set the standard against which those to follow are judged; the last one to present has the last word and can shine in comparison with what has gone before. The agencies in the middle are likely to stay there.

PRESENTATION DETAILS

Here are some timely tips that may help you. Generally, the more you use visuals to reinforce your key points, the better your presentation will be understood.

- If practical, use your own conference room for the presentation. You are familiar with where everything is, you are in control, and you're on home territory.

- If you present in the client's office, be sure you check out the size of the room, where light switches and outlets are, seating arrangements, and equipment. Look for things that could go wrong.

- If you are renting a hotel suite or meeting room there are many pitfalls to watch out for.

  True story: An agency arrived to make a pitch with a full array of projectors and dissolve units mounted on a large frame. When they got to the meeting room they found that the room was too small to take their equipment.

  - Check out the power situation. Where are the power outlets? Can your power cords reach them?

  - Is there piped-in music? Can you turn it off? Where do you turn it off?

  - Is there a telephone?

  - Is there noise from the meeting room next door (applause or amplified sound)? Be sure no disturbance will come through when you are presenting.

  - If you are using audiovisual aids, go in well ahead of time to set up and be sure that everything is working. Never leave equipment alone in the room.

  - Allow for Murphy's Law and be prepared. Bring extra extensions, projector bulbs, etc. Always have a contingency plan if the equipment fails.

  True story: An agency was making a presentation. During the audiovisual section the power went dead. Reason? There were no available power outlets in the meeting room so the extension cord was connected to an adjoining room. When the maid came in to clean the room, she pulled out the plug to get the wire off the floor. This kind of thing can happen!

PUT YOURSELF IN THE CLIENT'S SEAT

When pitching new business, it's still *Advertising 101*. The client asks, "What's in it for me?" Always see the presentation from his or her point of view. While clients are listening they are thinking:

- Will I look good to the rest of my company if I hire this agency?
- Can I really work with them? Chemistry *is* important.
- Does their program do what we want it to do for us?
- Will they follow through on all their promises and deadlines?

Don't keep talking about how great your company is; emphasize how you can be a true problem solver.

STEPS TO TAKE BEFORE THE PRESENTATION

The more you prepare ahead of time, the smoother and more professional your presentation will be. Here are some timely suggestions for what to do before the presentation.

- Get out your votes before the presentation. How? Call everyone on the decision committee. If you can meet with them over coffee, lunch, or a drink, so much the better. Ask them about their company. What challenges or problems is the client facing? Let them talk . . . become a friend. Find out what they are expecting from the agency—expressed in their own words. This will give you a basic theme or idea on which to base your presentation.

- From a personal point of view, learn about their backgrounds, their hobbies, any peculiarities. You may be able to use something you learn in your presentation.

- Send a letter ahead of time. Let them know how excited you are to have the opportunity to be presenting to them.

- How about sending a three-dimensional item? Here are some ideas—perhaps unsophisticated, but effective.

  - A toy train: "You'll see that we're on the right track with our approach."

  - A firecracker: "Yes, we're red hot—we have some explosive ideas to help improve your bottom line."

  - Chocolate candy (everyone loves chocolate), coffee beans, a periscope, and so on. Your business is creativity, so you can come up with some better ideas. The important thing is to send something! They'll remember you at the presentation.

- Prepare name tags for each person who will be at the meeting . . . or stand-up table tents. Watch your spelling of names and be sure titles are correct. Make the letters large enough so that everyone will be able to read the names.

- Set up welcome signs in the lobby or by the elevator, in front of your office . . . or wherever they will see it before they enter the presentation room.

- Try to visit with the client just before making the presentation. Leave the impression that you are exciting, creative, and that you want their business.

- As the old gag goes, "How do you get to Carnegie Hall?" Practice, practice, practice. Plan it out: who is in charge and controls the tempo? Who presents the strategy? Who presents the creative? Make sure everything is in sync and that your presentation is timed perfectly.

THE TOOLS

We have touched upon some of the tools that should be available to support a new business development program. Some of them may already be in hand, but there may be others that you have repeatedly thought of adding. Therefore, we will do a roundup of some of the basic tools and you can consider which of them you should have on hand.

Electronic Audiovisual Presentation

Here we are talking about a standing presentation that can be shown to visitors to your agency, used as an introductory element in all your new business presentations and used in connection with speaking engagements.

This presentation should be prepared in modules that deal with various aspects of who you are, what you have been doing, and how well you do it. The modules should be available as individual modules or in various combinations to create a selection of longer presentations structured to various audiences. Some of the modules might be the following:

- Status of the agency: size in terms of people and billings, how long in business, where offices are located.

- Areas of special expertise: covers business categories in which agency has greatest depth of experience. Describes how agency got this experience. This module may be broken down into specific categories of business that can be extracted for talking to a prospect in terms of his specific industry.

- Client list: current clients and how long served. Describes specifically what each client does . . . types of products or services marketed.

- Key people on agency staff: covers brief bio of each.

- Case histories: runs down successful programs/campaigns and details results. Shows ads and collateral developed to support the program, meet client expectations, and get results.

- Physical facilities: covers facilities such as test kitchens, video studio, special conference rooms, computerization for databases, or creative work . . . whatever is appropriate to that individual client.

- Awards and recognitions: includes awards for creativity, for ad performance.

- Civic support activities: shows pro bono work done for charities, public facilities, and community advancement and the results.

Videotape is one medium for such a presentation if the agency can afford the investment required to do a professional job. If your television work is significant, this medium is a must.

The alternative is computer presentations done on programs like Microsoft PowerPoint or Lotus Freelance Graphics. They allow the use of various optical effect transitions from one slide to another and provide the ability to "build" when presenting a list of points, i.e., bring them on one-by-one with varying effects. This is the nineties version of writing on the blackboard, but better, neater, and more interesting!

A third option is the old, tried-and-true 35mm slide show. This can be made more professional appearing by the use of two projectors and a dissolve unit that allows for a smoother change between slides.

Each medium has its advantages and disadvantages. For example, taped work is expensive to change and usually must be displayed on a relatively small monitor. Shows run directly off a computer have the same display problem. However, there is an answer to this, and that is to use an overhead converter, a unit that plugs into a desktop computer or laptop and is projected on the glass screen of an overhead projector, allowing projection onto a large screen. These units are relatively expensive, however, and definition is not as good as with slides.

The advantage of computer presentations is flexibility to change copy and illustrations.

Slide shows are less expensive to produce than tape and can be edited and modified easily. However, a two-projector show is unwieldy to transport and requires more set-up time. Slide shows preclude real-time action, but the illusion of action can be achieved with dissolves.

Presentation Card Library

Easel cards can be used for a simplified presentation—or to supplement a slide or taped presentation. These are best utilized to present a visual outline of the material being presented. For best effect, the copy on these cards should be typeset, rather than hand lettered. Mount them on foam plastic boards, which look good and are light enough to carry easily.

The card library should have a range of subjects similar to that discussed earlier under "electronic audiovisual presentation." A large number of case histories can be put on such cards, allowing the presenter to select those that are best targeted to the prospect being addressed.

Leave-Behind Literature

The typical agency brochure, as previously mentioned, is the standard leave-behind. However, this usually is so general in nature it doesn't target the prospect's particular interests. The most effective leave-behind should be some form of reproduction of the visuals in the presentation the prospect has been shown. One effective way to accomplish this is to photograph your slides or presentation cards and make color photocopies of them to give to the prospect.

If you have newsletters or thinkpieces that the prospect has not seen, select a few of the subjects that are most appropriate and leave some of these with the prospect. These may give him a further understanding of the agency's philosophies and strategies.

An alternative to leaving all these thinkpieces behind is to have one hand-delivered each day following the presentation up to the time the prospect makes a decision. The principle here is to stay top-of-mind without being a phone-call nuisance.

Caution: If you have done special research for a prospect, do not leave such studies with him following the presentation. If the prospect finds your work to be valuable, make him come to you. He gets the full reports if he hires your agency. If the prospect hires a competing agency, you have the option of offering to sell this work to the prospect.

WHAT DO CLIENTS SAY ABOUT AGENCY PRESENTATIONS?

Do you ever go back after a presentation and ask the prospective client you pitched for a critique of the agencies who presented? It's a good idea, but not often done. So, we've done it for you. Here is a compendium of comments we have picked up over the years.

Common Mistakes

"Most agencies want to show a creative idea or a new product idea. We are more interested in seeing a new marketing idea. We seldom do."

"Too many ad agencies spend too much time on trivia and not enough on simple homework."

"They didn't bring any creative people to the meeting."

"The best presentation we got was from a small outfit that showed us a terrific idea—a musical commercial. But when we asked what else they would do for us they were lost."

"Too much razzle-dazzle, not enough understanding."

"Too many agencies bring the wrong people to the presentation. Good salespeople, but not the people who will actually work on the account."

"It bothers us if the agency pitch is too structured, too tight. We think they can only do one kind of advertising. This happens when all their advertising looks alike . . . same graphics, same kind of headlines, etc."

"We are turned off by agencies that take a whole different approach to advertising than what we have done traditionally. They want to change everything—right off."

"We hate to see too much money spent. It is uncomfortable—especially when the ideas are way out in left field . . . no hope of ever using them. How they think is more important to us than how they make layouts and write copy."

"The ad agency that is interested in us ought to know something about us . . . where we sell, how we promote, where our ad money is spent, etc. This kind of homework is not too difficult. Too few do it."

"We liked one agency but thought that they were too unknown, too small, too risky."

"They showed too much creative work . . . commercials five years old. Didn't allow enough time for marketing and problem-solving talk."

"Brought too many people, tried to snow us with their manpower. Most of them had nothing to say. Slows down a meeting. Two or three people is enough for us. The *right* two or three."

"If there is any one serious handicap in most agency presentations to us, it is lack of knowledge about our business. We've had agencies tell us, 'We don't know your brands or much about your business . . . but we can learn that soon enough.'"

"Too many dull, routine pitches. They show their reel, brag about their people, show a few case histories—and expect us to stand up and cheer."

"A mistake we find that agencies make in their presentations is that they don't tell us what they can do for us. Instead, they spend all their time telling us what they have done for others."

"We look to see something new and different when an ad agency comes in. We hope to learn something: not free ideas, but what is happening in advertising—trends, new directions—maybe in marketing innovations. But, usually, it is the same old spiel."

"Over the years we have noted a lack of persistence in ad agencies seeking our business. One pitch and they quit."

"Speculative presentations: if they are elaborate it embarrasses us. Since some of us here have been on the agency side, we know how much they cost in time and money. Further, if they do much of this kind of selling, they aren't saving enough for their clients."

"Not being aware of client conflicts."

"Case histories in fields other than our own are boring. We know they are important to the agency's pitch but they should be done quickly and lightly."

"Overpromise the time of top management."

"Don't stress enough 'What's in it for Mr./Ms. client?'"

Favorable Comments

"The agencies that impress us most are the ones that have themselves all together . . . do a smooth, well-organized pitch. It reflects their way of doing business—how they might work for us."

"A lot of things are important: the people chemistry, the agency's track record, services offered, etc. But we put a lot of store in enthusiasm, too. In the long run, many agencies have all these. So, it gets down to a subjective choice, I guess. I just like them better."

"The thing that impressed us the most about the agency we selected was their knowledge of our business—frozen, packaged foods. We also liked the idea that the president of the agency (not a big shop) would be the main contact."

"We liked them because their presentation was shorter and more to the point."

"Enthusiasm, genuine interest, and excitement can make the final choice when everything else seems to be equal."

"To be honest, the decision between the final choices often has to do with the agency's reputation in the field. Top management feels safer with a well-known, often big agency, over a small unknown. If the middle management pushes hard for an unknown but good shop—it's got to have a lot of guts."

"They had a strong agency philosophy that gave us confidence and told us what they were all about."

"The operating heads of the agency are important in the first meeting. They have to assure us that they will take a close interest in our account, but the second echelon is important, too. We always listen closely to our product people and what they think of their opposite number at the agency."

"We gave one agency the account because it took up our offer to come back."

"The agency avoided an often-repeated mistake of other agencies. They took the time to find out what our people are like. You can't expose a long-haired freak to a redneck."

"We liked the fact that they were buttoned-down. They used checklists and had paid a lot of attention to details."

Summing It All Up

There is a pattern in these comments that should command the attention of all agency new business presenters. Note the following:

- Do your homework. Get to know your clients' business, people, history, and marketing communications viewpoints.

- Try to bring something new to the table. Prospects are looking for what an agency is supposed to provide: innovation and creativity.

- Show them the right people: both top management and second echelon. But don't overkill with too many people present.

- Take it easy with the "wonderful us" syndrome. Focus more on the client's situation and needs. Tell what you'll do for them.

- Get your act together. Put on a businesslike, well-organized, smoothly run show.

- Don't expect to get the business with a hit-and-run presentation. Follow up.

FOLLOWING UP

Each and every contact with a prospect that elicits any degree of interest should be followed up promptly. If your first approach by letter draws a reply, get on the phone right away and press to set up a personal meeting.

When you've been invited to make a formal presentation it's especially important to follow up to see if a decision has been made or if you can supply more information that would be helpful in reaching a decision. One good gambit is to ask if the agreement form you left with the prospect at the end of the presentation has been signed yet or whether it needs some modifications.

If your presentation hasn't brought in the account, it's important to try to find out who did get it and why you didn't. This won't get you the account, but it will help you profit by your mistakes and build a better presentation for the future. Who knows, you may even get a second crack later on at the guy who turned you down.

It's important to keep in contact with the prospect who has chosen another agency, because many things can happen after the appointment. Records show that when the relationship is not working, six months is the "magic period" when a client finally becomes unhappy with the agency and is ready to make a change. If you have continued to be active in your new business efforts during this period you will have a good chance to be appointed the agency. Stay with it.

—24—

Look Before You Leap

"Beware of strangers bearing gifts."

When an eager account executive wants to bring his "vest-pocket" account to your shop with no presentation, and it looks so easy, remember that the account can fly out the window just as easily.

How often have you heard the old cliché "There's nothing wrong with this agency that a million dollars of billing won't cure"? Sometimes that's true; but sometimes even that won't solve the agency's problems.

I think the general principle should be that any procedure that brings in profitable and desirable business is good, while activities aimed at increasing billing without these qualifications are likely to be bad. Perhaps you think this is an obvious statement; however, agencies frequently are so desirous of increasing their billing that they wish-think themselves into the conclusion that they make money on practically anything that comes in on top of present billing. This is very far from the truth.

VIEW SOME BILLING SKEPTICALLY

I'm referring to billing from clients who have a legitimate product or service to sell and whose financial responsibility is well established but who, for whatever reason, prefer to operate under unorthodox agency-client relationships. There are two basic types.

Controlled Accounts

Possibly the most common account of this type is a business controlled by individuals who peddle it around to agencies, placing it with the outfit that offers the best deal, without too much worry about the abilities involved or the appropriateness of the agency for the accounts concerned.

The smart salesperson who peddles this kind of account will tell you the billing is sure to be so many thousands of dollars, and he or she will do all the contact and creative work. All the agency has to do is check the insertions and send out the bills.

Soft pedaled or totally ignored at this time are the facts that the agency is taking a credit risk, that the peddlers will need office space, telephone service, possibly the part-time services of a secretary, and much more time from the other agency executives than is mentioned in the preliminary talks. Nothing is ever said about the real qualifications of the agency to handle the account involved or the possible discontent of the client if the advertising service delivered is not good. And you have no way of judging whether this peddler is a good advertising person or not.

Sometimes this kind of deal works out fine, but in general it is the least desirable new business the agency can get. It rests in one person's pocket; it stays only as long as it is more profitable to its controller than some deal offered by another shop.

Look with suspicion upon any split commission deal. It is generally undesirable from many angles. You have no real hold on any business you do not contact yourself and in which the agency is not functioning creatively.

Cut-Rate Accounts

These are another common cause of agency losses. All sorts of deals are worked out by which, in one way or another, the agency rebates a large portion of the commissions earned. Agency associations endeavored to outlaw the procedure, but were ruled to be in restraint of trade by the federal government.

Agencies, said the ruling, were free to sell their services at any price they considered fair. Consequently, many clients are shopping around and buying their agency services at bargain rates.

You are taking your business life in your hands if you get into any of these cut-rate situations. At cut prices you can't deliver proper services and dissatisfaction is sure to result.

Any deal that departs from the simple bilateral benefit agreement between agency and client should be looked at with suspicion. Basically the client has something to sell and an appropriation for selling it. Some part of this money may well be earned by the agency because of its specialized skills and its facilities for producing the advertising and placing it where it will do the most good.

But any working agreement that cuts down on the service rendered or that reduces the agency's legitimate profit is destined to fail. It is surprising how often this simple fact is ignored and how often arrangements are started that cannot possibly succeed.

When the client buys at cut rates, he never expects the same cut in service. That's invariably what he gets, however. You go all out learning about the client's business, spend far more than you should in time, hoping that it will pay off eventually, but you are so handicapped by too low an income that the client complains, out goes the account, and the whole operation nets you a serious loss. Far better to insist on remuneration higher than the 15 percent standard if the account promises to be difficult and requires excessive time to handle properly.

Sad to relate but true, it is almost invariably the agency left holding the bag in these deals and it is the agency that loses the money. Only the agency's capital is used. The client risks nothing financially, although lost sales and reputation may be far more expensive in the long run than has been realized.

SPECIAL PROJECTS AS A FOOT IN THE DOOR

In recent years it has become increasingly common for the initial agency-advertiser relationship to be in the form of a special project. Many agencies welcome this technique, which gives them a chance to show what they can do without committing the advertiser to an assignment of his or her whole account.

A good example of how this can benefit an agency was presented by a friend of mine in Texas who took on a special assignment for a local division of a nationwide multi-industry conglomerate. To do the job right he had to visit and work closely with many of the offices of subsidiaries and divisions. What better way to get to know the advertiser's people and gain their confidence? Another agency I know, in

Nebraska, got what are now its two largest accounts by handling specialized projects for them and impressing them with what it could do.

Of course, there are dangers in this approach, too. If an agency takes on a succession of special projects for a client, it may acquire the reputation, at least with that advertiser, of being a hotshot bull pen artist who's never given a starting assignment. And it's frustrating to be always putting out fires.

CREDIT CHECKS

This may seem redundant in a chapter on looking before leaping, but it's so vital to an agency's very survival that I'm going to say it again. Don't take any business from a client whose credit is doubtful, or, if there is any question about it, get your money before closing dates or other times when your liability begins. Never forget that it's your credit, your capital, and your reputation that are on the line.

THE EFFECT OF CLIENT CONFLICTS

The spate of megamergers in the mid-1980s among both agencies and advertisers has raised a considerable amount of worry in the agency business about client conflicts and the subsequent loss of business. That this is a real cause for concern can be seen from the large-scale client shifts that followed the Saatchi & Saatchi absorption of Ted Bates and the creation of Omnicom by BBDO, Doyle Dayne Bernbach, and Needham, Harper & Steers. According to stories in *Advertising Age,* the volume of billing that changed hands came to more than $372 million.

Some of the details of these account shifts show Saatchi/Bates losing $255 million net and Omnicom losing $117 million net. On the other hand, Young & Rubicam (not merged) gained $254 million net. This frantic activity contrasts sharply with total account shifts of $576.5 million in 1976 and $1.4 billion in 1981. This problem has continued in the nineties, as more and more "megamergers" occur.

This kind of account shakeout can be to your benefit if you are able to pick up one of the accounts being shed by the mergee. This situation raises two related questions. The first is how to minimize the effect of client conflicts on your agency whether they arise from a merger, from your acquisition of a new account, or from your client's entry into a business competitive with that of one of your other clients. In considering any question of client conflict you must remember that, just as beauty is in the eye of the beholder, a perception of conflict is always in the eye of the client. If he or she thinks it exists, it does whether you think so or not.

If the potential "conflict" results from your taking on a new account, just plain common sense indicates that you should clear with your present client before taking on a new account that might conflict with one of his or her areas of interest to ensure, as best you can, that it will not be considered a conflict. It will help him or her make this favorable decision if you have served him or her long and well on your present assignment and he or she is thoroughly convinced of your integrity.

Another positive step you can take to minimize the effects of a possible conflict is to provide that the two potentially conflicting accounts are handled by completely different groups in your office or even in a different office if you have more than one. Some mergers are designed with this possibility in mind.

If none of these efforts allay your current client's doubts, you may have to be willing to shed your current client if the new one offers higher billings.

The second question is whether you should seek out a merger in order to position yourself better to take advantage of this churning of accounts.

Before answering this second question, let's first consider the reasons why agencies seek to merge. These, not necessarily in order of importance, are: (1) financial, (2) acquisition of good people, (3) acquisition of new accounts, (4) acquisition of an office in a new territory, and (5) acquisition of a service capability you do not now have, such as direct response or medical advertising.

I would strongly urge you to seek out a merger only if it makes economic sense in view of the above goals. If merging would also help you meet possible conflict situations (for example, by giving you a completely separate office facility), that should be considered a plus value, not a strong reason in itself, for merging.

—25—

What Do Advertisers Look for in an Agency?

This seems to be a good note on which to conclude this section on new business. Certainly if we know what an advertiser is really looking for, we can prepare and deliver our presentations more intelligently.

Recently I was privileged to sit in on a seminar at which a group of advertising managers told how they had gone about selecting the agencies to which they had recently shifted their accounts.

The first thing each of them did was draw up a list of criteria applicable to his or her particular situation. Three were used by all of them. First, size in relation to his own advertising budget. Each of them was concerned that the agency neither be so large that his or her account would be lost in the shuffle nor so small that his or her account would put a severe strain on the agency's facilities and personnel. It's important to note that no client wants to be the largest account or the smallest account in your agency.

Second, location was a factor in all cases except one, which was located in a small city with no agencies of any size. All the ad managers wanted to be sure of getting service when they needed it. However, E-mail, faxes, overnight deliveries, and the like have made this criterion much less important.

The third common criterion was the experience of the agency. It needn't be in the advertiser's specific industry but should be related. For instance, a manufacturer of snack foods was interested in any kind of packaged goods background; a bank looked for experience with financial institutions other than banks; a manufacturer of products for the automotive aftermarket wanted experience in marketing brand name merchandise of any sort.

Information of this kind is pretty easy to come by from published sources and was used to narrow down to a manageable number the agencies to be considered.

Some agencies on the final lists may have been known to the advertiser from previous contacts, others by reputation only, but every one of them seemed able to provide what was wanted.

Interesting, isn't it, how these list-building criteria parallel almost exactly the considerations the agency uses in building its own file of likely prospects?

Thus, after narrowing the list of agencies to those he or she believes can do the job, the advertiser sets up a series of more or less formal presentations from each of them. Then he or she makes a choice, which has to be pretty subjective.

Whatever the rationale used by individual advertisers, I think the essential qualities of an agency on which the final selection is based are brain power, good judgment, experience, and intellectual honesty.

What tests can the advertiser apply that will indicate the presence or absence of these essentials in an agency under consideration?

INTELLIGENCE

The brain power of an agency, or intelligence, will show up in its type of presentation, its analysis of itself in relation to its future client, and its tact, foreshadowing happy or difficult personal relations to come. One of the participants in the seminar I attended put it this way, "Will this agency-client relationship be a good one four or five years from now?"

The client's response to evident agency intelligence will be, "We like these people. They speak our language. They probably will be able to understand our business. They think about our problems with good common sense. They are not bluffing. We can understand their reasoning."

Intelligence is most frequently tested by the agency's solutions to problems. All those indications listed above, when you think about them, are right or wrong answers to problems.

Intelligence is of surpassing importance as an agency asset. It means much more than cleverness, ingenuity, even more than selling skill. It is, in an individual, the ability to understand and cope with the difficulties of an environment. Selling is an exercise in understanding and coping with the buying environment. This term means whatever we are surrounded by. In our always expressive slang, whatever we are up against.

GOOD JUDGMENT

Let's turn now to good judgment. This depends largely on intelligence, but it goes further by also involving the understanding of people and the ability to interpret events. Essentially, in the agency-client relationship, good judgment will show up in recommendations regarding business policy. Here the advertiser must beware of the human weakness of considering as correct the judgment with which he or she agrees. The advertiser must be very open-minded in recognizing and giving proper consideration to judgments that differ from his or her own.

One of the seminar panelists selected his new agency when he felt he could answer yes to the question, "Would we have the guts to follow really significant, substantial, meaty recommendations from this person?" That the advertiser could even formulate this question to himself demonstrates clearly his conviction that the agency possessed good judgment.

EXPERIENCE

The next basic quality to look for is experience. By this I mean general business experience, not necessarily experience in the prospect's own business. Much might be said for the uncluttered mind that comes fresh to a business problem, without preconceived ideas based on "this is the way we have always done it."

Experience in advertising usually is demonstrated by materials illustrating what the agency has done for others. Here it is difficult to segregate the agency's contribution from that which may have come from the client. A series of case histories of accounts that have shown increased sales and bigger profits during the agency's tenure is as good an indication of agency experience as any. Mistrust any case histories of failures. They may or may not have been the agency's fault. Also mistrust the agency that, in its case histories, claims credit for every success the client ever had. Nobody is that good.

INTELLECTUAL HONESTY

And finally we come to intellectual honesty. Of all the forms of honesty, this is the rarest and most to be desired when one is considering an adviser. Monetary honesty we expect; individuals and corporations have learned it is dangerous not to practice it. Intellectual honesty is the ability to think straight and the courage to say what you think. It's the integrity to admit, for example, that extra media spending is not the answer to every problem.

When an agency demonstrates this kind of honesty a whole batch of possible minor faults can be discounted, for this is the most desirable and rarest trait in an adviser. When combined with intelligence and experience, it's the answer to an advertiser's prayer.

Many readers may accuse me of leaving out the desirable feature of compatibility. Well, it's nice to be married to a concern you like, with which you get along, and whose background and experience in life are akin to yours. It's much more important, however, for the agency to have the client's respect and to be able to give him or her real help.

What about creativity? Don't prospects look for evidence of that in an agency? I left it out deliberately because I don't think you can define creativity in terms that make sense at the time of a presentation. Just as the proof of the pudding is in the eating, the proof of creativity is in the results accomplished. And that's mighty hard to demonstrate in a presentation.

I don't think it's as important for the prospect to look for the ability to produce good advertising as it is to find the personal characteristics without which good advertising cannot be created. You do not, says the old English proverb, make silk purses out of sows' ears. It's quite possible that the client doesn't possess the ability to spot and appreciate good advertising. As a good businessperson, however, he or she should possess the ability to evaluate the human powers behind good advertising. He or she should pick an agency that evidently has brain power, judgment, experience, and intellectual honesty; he or she shouldn't try to think for it but leave it alone to give the best it can. The results of this philosophy should be a satisfying and rewarding relationship for both parties.

— Part VI —

Some General Observations

—26—

What It Takes to Succeed

Times have truly changed since Herb Gardner wrote this book. But basic human characteristics and what it takes to succeed have not changed. All through this book there have been suggestions on how to run an agency successfully. They cover a lot of different details, so it may be well to summarize here what I call the "10-Point Formula for Agency Success."

Here, based on a great many years of running and advising agencies, are the standards that, if strictly complied with by people whose characteristics and talents are as described, will be found to work.

HONESTY

Are you surprised to find this at the head of the list? Fact is, it is the single most important ingredient in the mix. This is because advertising agencies are trusted advisers to advertisers, who put large sums of money in the agencies' hands and have every right to expect that it will be expended properly. These advertisers ask for guidance in a difficult field, where many things are matters of conjecture, where results are far off in time and locale.

I'm not speaking of the alliances that last only a short time, but of those agency-client relationships that may last many years. (The short-term ones soon correct themselves.) Here, in these frequent and richly productive partnerships between the advertiser and the agency,

honesty on both sides is a must. Without it, the deal is doomed
almost before it starts.

ABILITY

No agency lasts long or has a chance for real success unless it knows
its business. An agency must be rich in creative ability, in marketing
savvy, in knowledge of people, in economics, and in a dozen or so
other things you can list as well as I.

Fundamentally an agency is hired and earns its gross income
because it knows more about these things than the client does, who
presumably has plenty on his mind understanding and mastering his
own business.

SELLING ABILITY

That means for the agency itself, and for the clients. This is a peculiar
and extrovert ability not all people or companies possess. You have to
understand folks and like them. You have to be able to put yourself in
their shoes. You have to have the arguments and the personality to make
someone else believe what you say and do what you recommend.

ATTITUDE

This means clients first, their interests before those of the agency. Of
course, agencies that possess this proper feeling toward the companies
that trust it with cash money will do credit to themselves without any
further effort. But this attitude is rarer than you might think.

MANAGEMENT

This, in the agency, means many things. It is concerned with the personnel of the agency, with financial matters, and with proper work
distribution and allocation.

Management manages both money and people. It has to have horse
sense. It has to look far ahead. It needs many attitudes quite foreign
to, and usually beyond, the abilities of creative and imaginative

advertising brains. It insists on knowing where it is going and how and when and often *why*.

It's easy to see why it is difficult for agency people to be good business managers. Fundamentally we are creative critters. We are salespeople. We are communicators of mercantile information and ideas. To do these jobs well we must be enthusiastic, able to put ourselves into the other fellow's shoes, and sympathetic and understanding of the reactions and attitudes of other people. These characteristics would seem to be almost diametrically opposed to those required of a typical, efficient business manager. So the functions of creation and those of management must always be performed by two separate people.

Because we're a people business, management of an advertising agency requires, either in the principals or in some associated individual, personnel handling as well as financial abilities. The person called on to function in these hard-boiled realities of figures and human reactions must possess good business judgment, extending to both events and personalities. He or she must be a good and accurate judge of facts and people. This individual must possess, most of all, good horse sense. He or she must be a realist par excellence. Lack of realism and common sense is one of the most frequent causes of agency failure.

MONEY

An agency needs enough to start with, including a generous margin of safety to provide for delays in payment and unexpected early setbacks (before it is familiar with these regular phenomena), enough to establish credit, take cash discounts, and most of all, avoid lying awake nights worrying where the payroll is coming from.

It needs to build this working capital out of profits and increase it steadily as the years go on and the financial jobs get bigger. It needs to invest surpluses wisely, so they earn their part in the gross income. It needs to pay its people well, not only today, but in the future also, when they will need more income.

ESCAPE HATCHES

Escape hatches are provisions against the unexpected. Agencies must set up ways to survive adversity. Some of these were covered earlier in the book. Continuously seeking new business, not extending credit, having sufficient working capital, hiring the right people, knowing where to buy outside services, and knowing what is going on in our industry are some ways we plan to survive hard times.

One of the most important reverses against which protection is needed is the all-too-frequent case in which the client cuts his budget, but doesn't reduce proportionately his needs for service. Agencies can adjust to this situation if given some time in which to turn around.

Two agencies I know have bought this time by including what they call "disaster clauses" in their client contracts. The first one (in a fee contract) reads:

> In the event the budget is reduced 10 percent or more, the Company agrees to continue, for a three-month period, the monthly fee which was in effect when the reduction was made. During this three-month period the Agency will adjust manpower requirements as necessary to provide the required service.

The second one (in all contracts) reads:

> Should the Client drastically reduce or cancel space contracts after approving the advertising schedules and after the Agency has done much of its work, the Client agrees to accept Agency billings in the amount of the commissions the Agency would have received for the schedules originally approved.

Adjustable Executive Capacity

This category really falls under management, but it is so seldom provided for that it rates a separate heading. What is meant is planning for and coping with the time, which always comes as the small agency grows, when one person's time and effort are inadequate to handle the growing responsibilities of more and bigger business.

Most agency heads are so busy working at their jobs that this contingency hits them unexpectedly, and they begin to run around wondering whether they should hire more people, merge with another agency, or provide on the shortest notice the most difficult of all commodities to find—able and experienced people.

These most important needs must be anticipated and provided for in advance. Second- and indeed third-string understudies should be in training continually. The wise manager always has a relief pitcher warming up in the bull pen.

CONSTANT NEW BUSINESS ACTIVITY

Most agencies begin to scurry around for business only when their billings drop or some account needs to be replaced. Part of the formula of every successful agency is constant selling of the agency itself, by mail, by telephone, by the Internet, or by any other means.

Unless you figure that account mortality is inevitable, you are in danger. Insist on agency growth, every year if possible, or know why not.

HAPPINESS

Run a happy shop that no one wants to leave, or your shop will leave you. Beat your people to the punch on all matters affecting their own welfare, particularly monetary. Especially in our sensitive, temperamental business this is of vital importance. Injustice, exploitation, too big a break for the boss, unkept promises—actual or implied: these are the cancers that spell death to any agency.

So, success (in the true sense of the word) boils down to ability, experience, and character.

—27—

Advertising Agencies and the Internet

By late 1995 it was clear that a major new business medium was emerging—the Internet. Within a matter of months the Internet, and its World Wide Web, became factors to be considered in advertising agency operational planning. This new medium offered potential for revenue generation at two levels. The first level was that of creation and placement of advertising on the Web for current clients. The second level was the use of the medium as a new business development platform.

While some agencies debated the need to develop their own Web site, others plunged in and took strong positions as factors on the Internet scene. In fact, many agencies opted to make the development of Internet home pages, and the placement and servicing of those sites, their primary business.

THE IMPORTANCE OF INTERNET PRESENCE

As most clients became cognizant of the Internet as a medium, it became essential for advertising agencies to stay in the lead relative to use of the Internet in the media mix. The alternative to agency involvement was noninvolvement and potential loss of client business to agencies that could handle this medium.

For those agencies without an Internet site, the question remains "Do we really need one and, if the answer is yes, what will it do for us?"

The answer is that there are many reasons for an agency to have an Internet site. The basic reason is that agencies must remain in the vanguard of marketing communications development, and failure to participate in the Internet can brand an agency as being behind the times.

If having an Internet site serves no other purpose than to provide a showcase of the agency's Internet site development capabilities, that alone makes it worthwhile. Even if the main use of the site is to show it during new business presentations, that is justification for having a site.

MAKING THE SITE WORK FOR YOU

The first rule in setting up an Internet site is: *make it interactive.*

The Internet is not a passive medium like newspapers, magazines, or brochures. Those who equate Web pages with magazine pages or brochures are missing the point. Those who enter a Web site are *participants.* They can engage in actions at the site or can communicate back to the site owners via E-mail facilities offered on the site.

Sites that are most successful offer contests, promotions, and two-way communication. Furthermore, the content of the site must be constantly renewed to keep Web users coming back. The action most likely to be generated by a passive site, which is predominantly text, is the visitor's exit to another, more interesting site.

An alternative to the fun-and-games approach to holding visitors is that of offering information of genuine value to the visitor. Many, perhaps most, Internet users are seeking information rather than amusement. Offer them specialized information and your site will hold their attention.

LEVELING THE PLAYING FIELD

One reason for the success of the Internet in attracting companies to develop Web sites is the fact that here is a place where the small operator can compete on a level with the large one. The cost of Internet participation is not so high that it precludes a small company from participation. The small agency may not be able to afford as many pages in its site as the larger one, but the number of pages may not be the key to establishing the agency as a player to be considered.

The content of the site can be the determining factor in positioning an agency. Because smaller agencies often have the creative talent to match larger agencies when it comes to one specific project, the smaller agency has the potential to develop a site that presents an appearance of top-level capability.

AN ALTERNATIVE TO DOING IT YOURSELF

But what if you determine that you cannot or should not try to do Internet pages with your current staff? The answer to this is obvious. You do just as you would when you want to augment your staff capabilities in art, copy, or production—you go outside. There are a multitude of operators providing Internet page creation and placement capabilities and they are looking for business. They would be glad to make an arrangement with your company to act as your Internet service division. When you have clients who want Internet service, they do the work and you take a commission (or set a price and mark it up for rebilling to the client).

You can link your Internet site to the home page of this provider. In your site you offer Internet service via your "affiliate" and provide a link button that will take the viewer into the outside provider's site.

FOCUS ON A SPECIALTY

Before developing a Web site, it is important to see what your competitors are doing. Surf through the home pages of other agencies and note the things they do in common. If everyone else is doing similar things, consider how you may differentiate your agency from the pack. For example, if your shop has special capabilities in ethnic markets, highlight that in your site. If your company has a record of successful promotions to specific audiences, feature that. If your agency has proprietary products, such as specialized databases or unique research studies, that should be your focus.

GETTING THE CONTACT

The challenge for your Internet site is to get the site visitors to make contact with your company. When they do make contact, you can add their names to your database of prospective clients and can begin a program of continuing contact with them.

—28—

How Agencies Tighten
Their Belts

The recessionary periods often change the way ad agencies do business. A lull in activity by clients and general business conditions, both locally and nationally (and sometimes internationally), send out a rude wake-up call.

At various places in this book, and particularly in the first section, I've discussed at length some of the characteristics of the advertising agency business that tend to make it a risky and unpredictable one—low profit margins, temperamental personnel, fickle clients, and so forth. At first glance, this might make it seem that advertising agencies would be particularly vulnerable in times of a decline in general business activity.

There are, however, a lot of characteristics of the agency business that tend to temper the effects of a recession on a well-managed agency with hard-working personnel. Here are some steps to follow.

What Successful Agencies Do to Tighten Their Belts

A recent survey of four hundred U.S. agencies conducted for *Advertising Age* revealed that an increasing number are relying on fee-based revenues, paying invoices later, and altering their business strategies.

Revenues from fees have grown more than those from media commissions and production. The respondents said their fee-based revenues had increased 45 percent since 1991 compared with a 32 percent increase for media commissions and 31 percent for production. This also shows that agencies are handling smaller pieces of business and have to move to fees because they can't cover their costs with commissions.

Another result of the recession: 76 percent of agencies report they've changed their strategic plans due to economic circumstances. The shifts can include increasing geographic operating area, adding product/marketing expertise, adopting vertical integration services, and forming strategic partnerships.

Many research reports indicate that those companies that keep up their advertising budgets during a recession maintain and even increase their share of market, while nonadvertisers fall behind.

Bottom line: smaller shops still live in a universe small enough that they can control their overhead. The much larger shops take another tack: they control their overhead by hiring and firing.

Providing a public relations capability should be an integral phase in the total marketing mix, both to serve clients and expand your ability to weather a recession.

AGENCIES SERVE A
DIVERSIFIED CLIENTELE

It's extremely unlikely that all parts of the nation's economy will be affected the same way or to the same degree in a recession. Recently, for example, fuel oil is down but coal is up; industrial trucks are up but materials handling equipment is down; refrigerators are down but freezers are up; beer is up and whiskey is down.

Most agencies have pretty widely diversified client lists and this gives them some degree of protection against disastrous declines in income. The members of First Advertising Agency Network, who typically represent small- to medium-size agencies, have between them clients in 379 of the 958 industries listed in the Standard Industrial Classification Manual. That's just under 40 percent of the total. What's more, the individual members serve clients in an average of 25 different industries. The chances of all, or even most, of these going sour at the same time are pretty remote.

As discussed earlier, here is another good reason to diversify your accounts and be careful of allowing one major account to dominate your shop. A good rule of thumb is to make sure that no account provides more than 20 percent of your gross income.

New Products Are Continually Introduced

In times of recession as well as in boom times American advertisers are forever adding new products to their lines. To realize the extent of this activity all you have to do is read the newspapers and magazines and note all the new improved products or the revolutionary advances in detergents advertised there. It is an exercise in futility even to try to compile a list that would be anywhere near complete.

Each of these introductions involves substantial amounts of advertising. The stories in *Advertising Age* carry such headlines as "HEFTY AD BACKING," "BIG BUDGET SET," "HEAVY PUSH," "HEFTY TV, RADIO EFFORT."

New Accounts Are Available

One of the hazards of the agency business that I pointed out in an earlier section is the frequent turnover in accounts. This is still a fact of life for agencies but it can be a source of hope as well as despair. Don't forget that every time an agency loses an account another agency gains one.

This switching of accounts goes on all the time—in good times as well as bad—maybe even more in hard times because some advertisers have an unfortunate tendency to fire an agency when sales fall off.

A smart, capable agency principal who runs a sound new business operation on a regular basis will undoubtedly gain more than he or she will lose in this kind of situation. The new clients are out there if you just keep beating the bushes.

A Record Number of Small Businesses Are Emerging

Latest statistics show that more employment is coming from the growth of small businesses than from any of the larger corporations that are downsizing at an alarming rate. This means new companies, new products, new marketing challenges, and, of course, new advertising expenditures. Look for new, emerging companies in your area.

Expenses Are Controllable

By its very nature most of the expenses an advertising agency incurs are variable and generally it has very little capital tied up in fixed assets.

All in all, the operating expenses of an advertising agency are highly controllable and can be reduced drastically if necessary to combat bad times. It may not be pleasant to scrimp and save and to work a lot harder than normal but it is possible, and most agency people would be glad to do it for the sake of survival.

Remember, with the accelerated use of faxes, computers, E-mail, computerized production, and fewer secretarial services, it now takes fewer staff to produce the same billing. Think about it when you may have to cut back.

Advertising Budgets Keep Increasing

As I discussed in the introduction to this book, throughout the years advertising expenditures have increased dramatically. And now with more and more acquisitions, megamergers, and agencies advertising internationally for clients, the projections are that advertising expenditures will continue to expand.

Conclusion

While the advertising agency business is not recession-proof, its basic nature is such that it can react to adversity much more rapidly and positively than can most businesses.

The total volume of advertising keeps on increasing steadily in good years and bad, and in this atmosphere there's business to be had by the smart, aggressive, well-managed agency even if it has to take some away from a competitor. Advertising is an intangible but vital factor in the business world; it is continually changing to meet new conditions, but, as an industry, it's in no danger of becoming obsolete and disappearing like the manufacturing of buggy whips. All in all, it's a business with great potential for the smart, sound agency professional.

It has become a marketing-driven society, and the old saw about "building a better mousetrap" just doesn't cut it any more. There will always be a need for marketing, advertising, sales promotion, and all the elements it takes to be successful in selling a product.

Welcome again to the brave new world of advertising. If you follow the principles of good financial management, and a solid new business program, you will do well. Good luck as you embark on one of the most exciting and rewarding experiences of a lifetime.

Index

About the Author

In 1955, Gene Hameroff started his one-man advertising agency, Hameroff & Associates in Columbus, Ohio, with no accounts and $250 working capital.

Over 35 years he built it into the top agency in Ohio, and according to *Advertising Age* it became the "third hottest agency in the U.S." The agency grew and became Hameroff/Milenthal/Spence, Inc.; it recently has been renamed H/M/S Partners, Inc., and now has six offices throughout the country with a gross billing of over $180 million.

Today, Hameroff's name is synonymous with advertising. He's seen it all, but hasn't kept it to himself. Through the years, he's taught advertising and marketing at Ohio State University and Franklin University, conducted marketing and advertising seminars for businesses, and coauthored a textbook, *How to Guarantee Professional Success*. With his partner, Pete Lustig, he formed Agency Management Publications and coauthored marketing tools such as the *Agency Tool Kit* and the working manual *66 Techniques—How to Slash Advertising Costs and Generate More Revenue* as well as now conducting seminars and on-site consulting throughout the United States.

He has been a friend and mentor to countless students and advertising professionals throughout the country.

Hameroff recently sold his interest in his agency and established EJH Consulting, Inc., in North Palm Beach, Florida. He now devotes his energies to doing what he loves to do best: helping smaller agencies grow and prosper. His insight and advice have helped many smaller agencies do just that.